LIVING A DREAM

LIVING A DREAM

LAUGHTER, PAIN AND LIFE ON THE APPALACHIAN TRAIL

Third Edition

Paralee Dawson-Hayward

Living a Dream
Copyright © 2013 by Paralee Hayward

Third Edition

All rights are reserved. No part of this book may be used or reproduced in any manner without written permission except for brief quotations used in reviews and critiques.

North Charleston, SC
www.CreateSpace.com

ISBN: 978-1482592764
       1482592762

Library of Congress Control Number: available for view

Printed in the United States of America

I have made every effort to trace the ownership of all copyrighted material and to secure permission from copyright holders. In the event of any question as to the ownership of any material, I will be pleased to make the necessary correction in future printings.

To order additional copies of this book, contact:

Gatewood Publishing
1-828-342-1656
paralee@outdoorhikerbooks.com
www.outdoorhikerbooks.com

Acknowledgments

Many people have influenced me and my work on this book.

Special thanks to each of the hundreds of men and women who have worked and are working so hard to maintain the Appalachian Trail.

I would like to offer my heartfelt thanks to all the trail angels who met us with cold drinks and snacks and left us with water when none was to be found. They shuttled us all over town to take care of all our needs, or opened up their homes to us and fed and sheltered us, and gave us the encouragement to continue.

Ed Hayward, the love of my life, for his patience and support during the planning stages and his encouragement when I was tempted to give up.

I would like to thank my sister, Lorelei "LaTripper" Schild, for putting up with me while we were out on the trail. Not every day was fun, and she helped me through the bad ones.

Brian Schneider, my nephew, who always had my mail-drops waiting for me when I arrived at my destination.

Mom and Dad, whose love of nature inspired me to take a big leap of faith and follow my dreams.

I appreciate the support from my many brothers and sisters, who had faith in me and encouraged me to follow my dreams.

My sister, Nachette, did a fabulous job deciphering my scribbled notes and typing them into my journal every week.

Janeen Schneider, my sister, is the author of some of the most inspiring poetry. Her words always give me a lift and can be found throughout my book.

The first steps you will take on the Appalachian Trail will be when you reach the summit at Springer Mountain in Georgia.

Springer is one of the few places in Georgia never forested, mostly because the ground is so rocky that trees don't grow well in the soil.

Follow your dreams one footstep at a time........

Table of Contents

ACKNOWLEDGMENTS **5**

INSPIRATIONS AND FEARS **11**

APPALACHIAN TRAIL **19**
- HISTORY AND FACTS 19

TRAIL NAMES AND ANGELS **23**
- TRAIL NAMES 23

PREPARATIONS **27**

PRE-HIKES **29**
- HARPERS FERRY, WEST VIRGINIA 29
- PINE GROVE FURNACE, PENNSYLVANIA 31
- CALEDONIA STATE PARK, PENNSYLVANIA 33

DAILY JOURNAL ENTRIES **35**
- GEORGIA 35
- NORTH CAROLINA AND TENNESSEE 43
- GREAT SMOKY MOUNTAINS NATIONAL PARK 52
- VIRGINIA: SOUTHWEST 74
- CENTRAL VIRGINIA 88
- SHENANDOAH NATIONAL PARK 109
- APPALACHIAN TRAIL IN SHENANDOAH NATIONAL PARK 109
- NORTHERN VIRGINIA 117
- WEST VIRGINIA 122
- MARYLAND 125
- PENNSYLVANIA 129
- NEW YORK AND NEW JERSEY 145
- CONNECTICUT 150
- MASSACHUSETTS 151
- VERMONT 152
- NEW HAMPSHIRE 155
- MAINE 157

SECTION-HIKER—LIFE AFTERWARDS **159**
- ABOL BRIDGE TO KATAHDIN CAMPGROUND, MAINE 161
- UNIONVILLE TO BEAR MOUNTAIN, NEW YORK 163
- BAXTER STATE PARK IN MAINE 172
- TESTNATEE GAP TO DICKS CREEK GAP, GEORGIA 176
- PENNSYLVANIA 179

    BAXTER STATE PARK AND KATAHDIN 181
    NEW YORK, CONNECTICUT, MARYLAND, AND PENNSYLVANIA 183

HEALTH AND FIRST AID 189

    FIRST AID SUPPLIES 190
    BUGS, TICKS, AND SPIDERS 190
    SNAKES 191
    ANIMALS 191
    WATER 192
    LIGHTNING 192

GENERAL INFORMATION 193

    SUGGESTED READING AND RESOURCES 194
    MAIL DROPS 195

GEAR, EQUIPMENT, AND FOOD 197

    HIKING BOOTS 198
    BACKPACK AND WATERPROOF PACK COVER 198
    SLEEPING BAG, COMPRESSION SACK AND MAT 199
    WATER FILTER 199
    CLOTHING 200
    FOOD 201
    STOVE AND COOKING SUPPLIES 202
    TENTING 203
    EXTRA SUPPLIES 204

MEMBER-MAINTAINING CLUBS 205

    APPALACHIAN TRAIL CONSERVANCY 205

APPALACHIAN TRAIL UPDATES 213

    GREAT SMOKY MOUNTAINS NATIONAL PARK 214
    HURRICANE SANDY IMPACTS 214
    VANDALISM 215
    GEORGIA 215
    NORTH CAROLINA 216
    GREAT SMOKY MOUNTAINS NATIONAL PARK 216
    NORTH CAROLINA & TENNESSEE BORDER 217
    SOUTHWEST VIRGINIA 218
    CENTRAL VIRGINIA 219
    SHENANDOAH NATIONAL PARK 219
    NORTHERN VIRGINIA 220
    WEST VIRGINIA 221
    MARYLAND 221
    PENNSYLVANIA 222

NEW JERSEY 223
NEW YORK 224
CONNECTICUT 225
MASSACHUSETTS...226
VERMONT 226
NEW HAMPSHIRE 227
MAINE..228

FINAL THOUGHTS **231**

ABOUT THE AUTHOR **233**

The Approach Trail to Springer Mountain in Georgia

Explore, Learn, Enjoy

Inspirations and Fears

Living a Dream is a true story of my desire to hike the Appalachian Trail in one continuous hike. My story shares the laughter, pain, and day-by-day life on the Appalachian Trail. This is not a story on how to go backpacking but on how to live life to its fullest. If you are willing to forgo modern conveniences for a little while and are able to endure a few aches and pains, the rewards are worth it all. For no other way can you experience nature in all its aspects.

Before I begin my story, I would like to share some of my inspirations for taking on such a big endeavor.

I grew up in the country and am one of twelve children, which is quite a story in itself. We spent a lot of time in the outdoors, trying to entertain ourselves. I have always tried to incorporate nature into myself. At times, I would find myself lying on the lawn and just gazing up at the clouds for hours, making the shapes of the clouds come to life. If we wanted to go visit our friends on the weekends, we would walk or ride our bikes. Half of the fun of getting together with my friends was the walk through the country getting there.

I have always enjoyed the freedom that camping allowed me to experience. I always tried to find the most remote area in the park and embrace the solitude as I would watch the squirrels scurrying around in preparation for winter, hear the lonely cry of the loon floating along out on the lake, or just listen to the gurgling brook as it lulled me to sleep. There is nothing better than waking up in the morning to the singing of the birds and the raw beauty of nature all around me.

I started reading the journals of hikers as they traversed the trail, and I could feel the tug to be part of it all.

I was inspired by a story about Emma Caldwell Gatewood, better known along the trail as Grandma Gatewood. She was the kind of personality about whom legends grow.

The following stories about Grandma Gatewood and Earl Shaffer were taken from the book Hiking the Appalachian Trail, Volume One, First Edition, published by Rodale Press, Inc., in 1975.

Grandma Gatewood climbed Katahdin for the first time in July 1954. At the time, she was in her late sixties, and had borne eleven children. When she reached the summit, she put on a black wool sweater from her pack in which she carried her belongings and ate a lunch of raisins while she counted the lakes and ponds below. When she reached one hundred, she gave up counting, even though other ponds could be seen on the horizon.

She was the first woman to walk the entire Trail in one continuous trip, and all alone, straight through from one end to the other. In 1956, at the age of sixty-seven, and 145 days later, she climbed Katahdin for the second time. For her hike, she had fashioned a backpack out of denim material. Grandma Gatewood's pack seldom weighed more than twenty pounds.

Seventeen months later, Grandma was back on the Trail in Georgia. In September of 1957, she completed her second hike along the Appalachian Trail. She went through six pairs of Keds shoes on this trip. She set another record and was the first person, man or woman, to hike the entire trail two times. She said, "I wanted to see some of the things I missed the first time."

In 1958, the year after her second completion of the Trail, Grandma began a series of walks along the Trail. In 1964, at the age of seventy-seven, she finished what she had begun ten years earlier. She continued on to walk the Knife Edge Trail from the summit of Katahdin.

Grandma Gatewood also tested her agility on other footpaths. There was the Long Trail in Vermont, parts of the Horseshoe and Baker Trails in Pennsylvania, the Chesapeake and Ohio Canal Towpath Trail in Maryland, and others. She also walked the Oregon Trail in 1959 at the age of seventy-two as part of the hundredth anniversary of the Oregon Trail.

A Boy Scout leader summed it all up by saying, "Grandma, you've broken all the rules for hiking—but you got there just the same."

Grandma Gatewood passed away on June 5, 1973. She was eighty-five years of age and had lived a very full life.

Another motivator was Earl Shaffer of York, Pennsylvania who became the first verified thru-hiker in 1948.

During Earl's hike, the Trail was extremely primitive; therefore, it took Earl 124 days to hike the entire Trail. Seventeen years later, when he was forty-five, he hiked the Trail again, starting at Katahdin and going south. He completed the AT in ninety-nine days. In addition to being the first person to walk the Trail in one continuous journey, Earl was also the first person to walk the entire Appalachian Trail both directions.

I was so inspired by Bill Irwin's story I thought I should include it. I found the following article in the Power for Living issue dated September 30, 2007. If you are looking for an inspirational or keynote speaker who knows challenge, change, courage, and success, Irwin is certainly the man for the job.[1]

---

[1] Photos of Bill Irwin and article about his hike provided and approved by Alice Cary, Freelance Features, and Bill Irwin.

Irwin had never been backpacking or hiking in his life. He knew nothing about the Appalachian Trail. Physical fitness really hadn't been a priority for him. And as a fifty-year-old blind man, he didn't have a desire to go walking along a rugged path just for the thrill of it. Yet, eight people who didn't know Irwin—and didn't know each other—independently phoned or wrote to him. Each told him they felt impressed to challenge him to try to hike the Trail. None of these people had any Christian beliefs, but as a relatively new Christian, Irwin sensed that God had prompted these strangers to make the same pitch for a purpose.

So, after he jettisoned various excuses for not hiking, Irwin agreed to give it a shot. He figured he could make two or three miles and satisfy his encouragers.

Irwin didn't quit after a few miles. He didn't even give up after a few days. Despite the tremendous difficulties he encountered, Irwin spent eight months walking the entire Trail. The blindness added weeks to the journey, which is completed by only about 200 people each year. Family and friends accompanied Irwin at the beginning and near the end of his adventure. But for about eight-five percent of the journey, Irwin walked alone, except for his German shepherd guide dog, Orient.

During the walk, every morning before he began, he would listen to an audio cassette tape from his son Billy, describing landmarks he would encounter that day.

He lived in Burlington, North Carolina, at the time, and members of his Sunday school class mailed him food supplies along the way. Various sporting goods and hiking equipment companies took care of outfitting him for the trek.

A challenge for Irwin—or for anyone who attempts the Trail—is coping with the rugged terrain. He had to climb cliffs, cross bridges, and ford streams.

The first two hundred miles are uphill. And then he had to deal with adverse weather conditions.

As he embarked on March 8 from Springer Mountain in Georgia, Irwin still had to contend with remnants of Hurricane Hugo from the year before. Along the first hundred miles, Irwin kept encountering downed trees and other debris that hadn't been cleared.

Occasionally, he lost time because he wandered off the path. Plus Orient had to spend several days resting because of injured feet.

During spring and fall, Irwin endured an inordinate amount of rainfall. During the summer, he battled hot drought conditions. Every day in October, along the path, Irwin felt rain or snow. For the final 300 miles, Irwin struggled to keep his footing on ice and snow.

When floodwaters washed out a bridge, Irwin ended up being carried under by the current and nearly drowned. He also broke a rib and became hypothermic. On average, he fell about twenty-five times each day. Yet he kept going, because he believed God would be glorified. On November 21, after walking through fourteen states, Irwin completed his journey at Katahdin in Maine.

By the end, Irwin understood why God wanted him to make that journey in 1990. In becoming the first, and to this day, the only blind person to hike the Appalachian Trail, Irwin generated more publicity that year in the United States than anyone except for President George Bush. Irwin granted interview after interview—on the condition that the writer mention God as his motivation for hiking.

Irwin is now a very celebrated motivational speaker.

Ed and I have always taken the road less traveled, and this has always made such a difference in our lives. I made my final decision to research and prepare for my hike while spending the summer in Alaska.

I had never seen such a natural, untouched wilderness anywhere in the United States.

I just felt as if I could pitch my tent and spend the rest of my life there. I was such a free spirit in Alaska. I never worried about the time of day or what day it was. I just took each day moment-by-moment and enjoyed being a part of such a beautiful, unspoiled wilderness. I felt like a free spirit, ready to spread my wings and fly. I thought I could experience that type of freedom while hiking the Appalachian Trail.

Everything I do or feel has been in some way influenced by the natural scene. My life with Ed has been a world so few are lucky enough to live in—one of peace and beauty. I enjoy being a part of peoples' lives, their future, and their fate. There is so much beauty in this world to be seen, and what better way to see this than a daily hike through this country without life's interruptions. I planned on being a changed person forever at the end of my hike.

I knew, before I ever took my first footstep on the AT, that it would be a physical challenge for me. I was fifty-six years old when I began my hike, and my sister was forty-nine. I left for the trail with a brace on both knees. I had already had surgery on one knee and knew it could be the one thing that could restrict me from finishing the entire trail. I also have a history of back and neck pain and have had surgery on my neck as well. I was concerned about carrying a thirty- or forty-pound pack on my back.

There have been others in their eighties who started and finished their hike, so I thought, Why not a crippled-up old lady in her fifties?

Over the years since I hiked the trail, I have had tremendous interest from friends and family who wanted to hear more about my journey.

I decided to share my journal with others, and after much research, I have included some facts as well as the history of some of the areas I have come to love along the trail. The following is a day-by-day journal of my adventure. At night, while in my tent, which was like being in a cocoon where you can barely sit straight up, I would scribble away, trying to recapture the day's events. I was sometimes so tired that all I could think of was falling asleep.

I never missed a day of writing while I was out on the trail. Some days, I couldn't write enough about the beauty around me, and other days, I might just write a few words. I don't claim to be a writer, just a dreamer who wants to share the story of her life on the trail. I didn't edit my journal fully because I was afraid it would change what I was experiencing at that moment.

My story includes the tedious process of preparing for a thru-hike along the AT. I thought that if I shared my basic preparations, experiences, and resources, it would help to inspire future hikers to follow their dreams, whether it might be a thru-hike or just section-hike of the trail. I met a man at Katahdin Campground in 2007, and he had been section-hiking for ten years and was just finishing the entire AT with his summit up Katahdin. His excitement to have completed the entire trail was as exhilarating as hiking it from Georgia to Maine in one continuous trip.

I have included my gear list, mail drops, pre-hikes, and other resources I hope you find helpful while you are planning your hike.

I left for my hike with several fears and concerns. I have always been afraid of heights and knew I had several mountains to climb. You are very exposed and above tree line on many of them. I was aware, from some of my pre-hikes that I would be traversing through very rocky, slippery, and muddy terrain with exposed roots that could trip you in a flash. I was terrified of falling and being alone for days before someone found me.

I have a healthy respect for bears and snakes, but the fear of meeting one on the trail scared the daylights out of me. I was encouraged to be prepared for the mosquitoes, the no-see-ums, and the black flies, especially in the New England states.

I had never hitchhiked before but knew that at times, that was the only way I would get to town for my mail drops, shower, laundry, and food supplies. I felt safer having my sister with me, and from everything I have read, I don't recommend hitchhiking if you are a woman hiking alone. You should do a little research since some states don't allow you to hitchhike. Go with your gut feelings.

Outdoor recreation experts have been inundated with questions about trail safety ever since hiker Meredith Emerson was abducted and subsequently murdered in the Northeast Georgia Mountains. At Amicalola Falls State Park, located near the starting point of the trail, resource manager Elisabeth Pinion said the recommendations for hiker safety haven't changed. "Be aware of your surroundings, and have a plan in the back of your mind," she said. "If you come upon a situation where you are uncomfortable, try to hike out with other people, if you can."

Many hikers go into the wilderness specifically to enjoy the solitude, and they prefer not to have a partner. In that case, you should always let someone know about your itinerary and when you plan to be back.

I think people who don't hike believe there's something to fear out in the wild, when it's actually a thousand times more dangerous in the city. Follow your gut feelings. If you don't feel safe hiking alone, take someone with you. Use common sense if you plan to hitchhike. Use shuttle services whenever possible. Carry a cell phone if it makes you feel more comfortable knowing you can reach someone in case of emergency. Do whatever it takes to feel safe, and just take time to enjoy being in sync with nature.

Kim "Sketcher" Sevy, a 2012 thru-hiker made this sketch of my boots in a matter of minutes. I picked Sketcher, Chaco, and Sherpa Mom up at Nantahala Outdoor Center and brought them home for a break. Before I dropped them off at the Trail the next day we went zip-lining at NOC. I hiked out with them for a few hours and said my goodbyes before heading back.

Appalachian Trail

HISTORY AND FACTS

The Appalachian Trail is all about inspirations and dreams.

The origin of the Appalachian Trail can be traced directly to Benton MacKaye. In 1921, MacKaye published in the Journal of the American Institute of Architects an article entitled "An Appalachian Trail, a Project in Regional Planning." Benton MacKaye introduced his idea of having a footpath that wandered along the Appalachian Mountains, a footpath that started in Georgia, at Springer Mountain, and ended in Maine when you complete the climb up Katahdin. With much determination, his dreams finally became a reality.

The Harriman family donated Bear Mountain State Park in New York, and the first sections of the Appalachian Trail were constructed in this park. With the help of many volunteers, the first section of the AT was cut on May 21, 1921, and dedicated in 1922. By 1933, the development of the trail was well underway in most areas except in Northern New England. A trail through Maine would have to traverse a remote region, giving rise to difficult access and maintenance problems. It was thought that the northern terminus of the AT should be at Mount Washington in New Hampshire. The entire trail was completed on August 8, 1937. The total length of the AT is now 2,176.2 miles. The numbers change often in order to avoid coming too close to civilization or because of acts of nature. There were massive forest fires in some sections of the trail in 1999, which caused it to be rerouted again.

The trail begins at Springer Mountain, Georgia and ends at Katahdin, Maine. The AT wanders over many mountaintops and along ridgelines, valley floors, ravines, wildflower meadows, and cow pastures. It passes through fourteen states, which include Georgia North Carolina, Tennessee, Virginia, which is twenty-five percent of the entire Trail., West Virginia, Maryland, Pennsylvania, New York, New Jersey, Connecticut, Massachusetts, Vermont, New Hampshire, and Maine.

The Southern Appalachians section of the trail, from Georgia to northeastern Tennessee, penetrates several of the vast national forests of the South and crosses the trail's highest mountain, Clingman's Dome, in the Great Smoky Mountains National Park. Though mostly well-graded, the trail through this section is remote, with long, strenuous climbs. The high ridges along the North Carolina and Tennessee borders are prone to winter-like weather, which is similar to parts of New England.

The Virginias section, between the panhandle of West Virginia and the Tennessee border, runs along the Blue Ridge of Virginia and the Great Valley of the Appalachians. This section includes portions of Harpers Ferry National Historical Park, Shenandoah National Park, and the Blue Ridge Parkway. Hiking is moderate to strenuous, and the southern part offers long, solitary stretches.

The Mid-Atlantic section is between eastern New York and central Maryland. This section runs between the glacial hills of the Hudson Highlands and the northern reaches of the Blue Ridge Mountains. It follows long, rocky ridges only a few thousand feet above sea level. Hiking is moderate, but parts can be very rocky and strenuous.

The Southern New England section of the trail travels through eastern Vermont and along the New York and Connecticut borders. Much of this section runs along glacier-scraped mountain ridges, such

as the Green Mountains and the Berkshires, and rocky New England river valleys. Though less strenuous than the northern section, it offers a challenging hike through deep forests. It's also within easy driving distance of major cities such as Boston and New York City.

The Northern New England section includes central Maine and western New Hampshire. This section offers some of the most rugged hiking and most challenging weather conditions of the entire AT. The path is often steep, rough, and slippery. Parts of it are above the tree line, where weather is especially severe. It includes Katahdin, the trail's northern terminus in Maine, the wild country of the One-Hundred Mile Wilderness, the Mahoosuc Range, and the White Mountains.

Exclusively, volunteers from thirty-one local clubs maintain the trail. Each club offers material that will assist you while planning your hike and while out on the trail. According to the Appalachian Trail Conservancy, there are approximately four thousand five hundred volunteers maintaining the trail. My sister and I volunteered in Massachusetts for one week, doing trail maintenance before we started our hike. It's very hard work but much appreciated by all the hikers. Our job was to assist in building rock steps up a very steep section that was becoming eroded from all the foot traffic.

The primary method for marking the Appalachian Trail is using a two-inch-by-six-inch rectangular blaze of white paint usually placed at eye level. Two blazes, one above the other, will indicate a change in direction of the trail. Most of the side trails are marked with a blue blaze. Most times, the blazes are within view of the last one. The volunteers do a wonderful job of keeping them visible.

Three of the highest peaks you will climb are Clingman's Dome in North Carolina at 6,643 feet, Mount Washington in New Hampshire at 6,288 feet, and Katahdin in Maine at 5,267 feet.

National scenic trail is the official designation for one type of trail protected by the national Scenic Trails System Act of 1968; the AT is a national scenic trail.

National Parks along the Appalachian Trail

- Chattahoochee National Forest in Georgia•
- Nantahala National Forest in Georgia•
- Pisgah National Forest in North Carolina•
- Cherokee National Forest in North Carolina•
- Great Smoky Mountains National Park in Tennessee and North Carolina
- Jefferson, George Washington, and Shenandoah National Parks in Virginia
- Green Mountain National Forest in Vermont
- White Mountain National Forest in New Hampshire

It's estimated that three to four million visitors hike a portion of the trail each year. Most enjoy day hikes and short backpacking trips, but each year, a small fraction of those hikers complete the entire trail. How many? Since 1936, more than ten thousand hike completions have been recorded by the Appalachian Trail Conservancy. This includes thru-hikes, multi-year section-hikes, and more than three hundred hikes by people who have already completed the AT one or more times. We call all these hikers "two-thousand milers."

Trail Names and Angels

TRAIL NAMES

A trail name is a badge of identity or individuality. They show that you are being accepted into the club. You're free to become someone you always wanted to be. It will more than likely cause a few laughs along the way. Trail names along the AT caught on in the late '70s, when the number of hikers increased dramatically.

I thought it would be fun to interview hikers each time I would go back out on the trail and find out just how they inherited their trail names.

I chose Trapper Lee for my trail name prior to hitting the trail because I was afraid I would get tagged with a name that would follow me the rest of my life. Ed's nickname is Trapper, and my legal name is Paralee, so I wanted to be known as Trapper Lee while I was out on the trail. I felt this would be a way I could carry Ed close to my heart while I was hiking along. Maybe I wouldn't miss him as much. Many of my friends still call me Trapper Lee. I have acquired several other trail names through the years as I have been completing my section hikes. I became Knee Bracer on my hike in Georgia because I kept giving out knee braces to the thru-hikers if they were experiencing knee problems. In Pennsylvania, Grayson and Tweety named me the Jolly Green Giant. They said that when I hopped from rock to rock with my long legs and green pants, I looked like a big green giant.

My sister, Lorelei "LaTripper" Schild, who was hiking with me, has a history of tripping and falling in her everyday life. We thought the name was appropriate, and she agreed it would be better than having someone else give her a nickname she might have to live with for the rest of her life.

Greg Benkert, known as Big Red, completed his thru-hike in 2002, and I would see him along the way with both knees taped up and struggling along. I had the pleasure of hiking from Abol Bridge to Katahdin Springs Campground the day before his summit up Katahdin. Jagged and her husband Tom, Tweety and her husband Greg Sr., Greg Jr., and his wife hiked with us that day.

Jeff, the Wanderer, was hiking along with his two friends Bill, The Yankee, and Tom, The Slack Packer, when they became separated from Wanderer. They often hiked alone, but when Yankee and Slack Packer arrived at the shelter, Wanderer was nowhere to be found. After a few hours, The Yankee and his dog, Dodger, went searching. They kept at it until 10:00 p.m. without any luck so they returned to camp. In the meantime, Wanderer realized he had wandered off the trail. Since it was getting dark, he decided to pitch his tent in the woods for the night. Slack Packer went out searching at 6:00 a.m. and was unable to find him. They decided to pack up and head up the trail. At about 10:00 a.m., they found Wanderer. I heard several similar stories of previous hikes they had done together when Wanderer had a habit of getting separated from the group.

I hiked with Lois Heald, known along the trail as Grayson, in 2002; and she told me she named herself after Grayson Highlands State Park, Virginia, which is her favorite place to hike.

Wilma "Chilly Willy" and her husband Ray "Just Ray" hiked in 2002 also, but I never heard how their names originated. We have stayed in touch with them through the years since our hike. They continue to go out each year and hope to someday complete the trail.

I also hiked with Leanne "Tweety" Linsmeyer in 2002. Her hiking buddies named her Tweety because the Crocs she was wearing at the end of the day were a bright yellow, the color of Tweety Bird.

At the last minute, before heading out for six months, Buzz decided to shave her head before she left for the trail; that way she wouldn't have to shampoo or style her hair. Most hikers don't carry shampoo because it adds to the weight in your pack. I never did hear what her real name was.

Season "Poetry in Motion" Chandler, Sky Blue Night, Possum, and Beach are a few of the 2002 thru-hikers whom I hiked with occasionally or would hang out with at the shelters.

Sofa King's brother named him after he had back surgery and was lying around on the sofa, recuperating. Two surgeries later, he has beaten all odds and is hiking and trying to complete the entire trail. I met him during my hike in Pennsylvania in 2008. My sister and I hiked with him and Steeler for several days and enjoyed the laughs and stories we shared around the campfire.

Steeler is from Pennsylvania and loves the Pittsburgh Steelers. I never did hear what his real name was.

Vino was once a thru-hiker who is now section-hiking. He carries food and wine and gives it to other thru-hikers. Before you know what he is up to, he will ask a hiker if they are thru-hikers. If the answer is yes, they will receive their wine and snacks as a reward. I also met Vino during one of my hikes in Georgia in 2008.

I love this one, Big Daddy Duct Tape. Everything on him seems to be held together with all colors of duct tape. It made me think of the song Coat of Many Colors.

I was hiking a section in Georgia when I met Snake Gripper, who was from Atlanta and had never backpacked before. He told me he was trying to hike the entire trail and was working for money and shelter as he went along. He started his hike in Georgia with his dog he had just gotten from the pound two days prior to his hike. He was planning on roughing it so he had very little gear. He carried dry rice that he would crunch on dry until someone offered to heat him some water to cook it in. He didn't have a tent, sleeping bag, stove, or water filter. He stopped at Neel's Gap and bought two foil emergency blankets. The story he told us is that one day, he was running out of food and saw a black snake in the trail. He caught it and cooked it for supper that night. His middle name is actually Gripper, so a hiking buddy named him Snake Gripper.

I met Signage on my hike up Katahdin in 2008. She was just completing her thru-hike with her summit up Katahdin. She was given her trail name because she was always looking for and reading the signs that tell you where the shelter, water, and towns are.

For Gordon "Old Man" Gamble, a retired AT&T engineer, hiking the trail was a dream nurtured for fifteen years until retirement made it possible. Old Man used the time wisely, planning his thru-hike meticulously to ease the stress on his frail, sixty-six-year-old body and arthritic knees.

My grandson, Tyler "Silent Bob" Towns, hiked with me the summer of 2008 and acquired his name the first night on the trail. We stopped at Graymoor Spiritual Life Center for the night and stayed in the pavilion at the ball park. Tyler was so engrossed with the activities around him that he was just quietly taking it all in. A few of the hikers befriended him and tagged him with the name Silent Bob. He now proudly tells everyone that his trail name is Silent Bob, but there is no Jay.

The same night we stayed at the Graymoor Monastery, I met Steve "Chaco" Chase and Sheila "Toe Socks" Black. They were both hiking in Chaco's, and their socks had toes in them. During their hike in 2007, Toe Socks fell and broke her leg. They were off the trail for the remainder of the year and were back out in 2008, attempting another hike. Shortly after I met the two of them, Toe Socks was diagnosed with leukemia and was off the trail again. One year later she lost her battle. Chaco completed his thru-hike in 2012 carrying Toe Socks ashes on his way to Katahdin.

The term "trail magic" was coined by thru-hikers to describe small, unexpected, remarkable events that lifted a hiker's spirits and inspired awe or gratitude. Trail magic came in two forms—the magic created by nature and the magic created by the kindness of strangers. Nature might offer magic in the glimpse of a black bear and her cubs or a hailstorm that held off until the safety of a shelter was reached. Acts of kindness by strangers might include a family in a state park, offering to share its picnic with a passing hiker, or a trail neighbor handing out cookies to hikers on a road walk.

For thru-hikers, trail magic is such a memorable part of the AT experience that they often return to the trail and create more magic for the next year's thru-hikers, often by handing out food and drinks or leaving it along the trail.

Preparations

There are several data books I found most helpful in planning my hike and while I was out on the trail.

I used the Appalachian Trail Thru-Hikers' Companion, along with the Appalachian Trail Data Book, to help me prepare my mail drops. The Data Book is a very concise and compact book that will fit in your pack without adding excessive weight. The Appalachian Trail Conservancy publishes both these books.

I carried The Thru-Hiker's Handbook by Dan Wingfoot Bruce. Wingfoot has been publishing the handbook for the past seventeen years and has decided to retire in 2008. Bob McCaw will be assuming the responsibilities of updating and publishing the book each year. This book is no longer available.

It contains detailed information about shelters, campsites, water sources, and other important trail facilities along this long footpath. You can also find the latest available information about places in nearby towns used by thru-hikers for rest and re-supply—the inside scoop on hundreds of preferred hostels, campgrounds, motels, restaurants, grocery stores, Laundromats, outfitters, and other services.

I was recently introduced to David Miller's book, Appalachian Pages. Each page has a topographical map of that section. I find that helpful when you are planning the next leg of your hike.

These are all very detailed books and should be considered as part of your gear whether you are planning a thru-hike or just section-hiking. Since every ounce is so crucial, I chose to separate my books and only carry the pages I needed for that week. The rest of the book was dissected and placed into my mail drops.

I did not use maps while hiking even though my sister liked to use them each night when planning for the next day. I did find them very helpful while planning my mail drops and calculating estimated daily miles.

Some of the data books include personal interest information that includes plants, animals, flowers, transportation to the trail, hiking equipment, personal safety, and wind-chill charts.

Most of the maintaining clubs have guidebooks and maps available for their section of the trail. One example is the Guide to the Appalachian Trail in Maine. This book includes seven maps. This is published by the Maine Appalachian Trail Club, Inc. The maps include topographic views showing the alignment of the trail and an elevation diagram showing the vertical relief of the trail. Most of the maps will show the shelters, campsites, and water supplies along that section of the trail. Most of the above resources can be found at a good outfitter's store, on the Internet, or through the Appalachian Trail Conservancy.

When planning your thru-hike, start with a high estimate for expenses. You could spend anywhere from $5,000 to $6,000 for gear, clothes, food, maps and books, and any other resources you may deem necessary. Part of this expense will be for hotels, hostels, and meals while in the trail towns.

I only have six months to go before I begin my long-distance hike. I can't believe that we are almost there. My sister and I have been planning this for so long now. I didn't realize how much work was involved. I'm still in the process of planning the mail drops for the six months I will be out on the trail. I have most of my gear ready to go. I will be working through the winter and taking the month of March off to finish preparing and to do some hiking, with a full pack, to prepare myself for the big hike.

I don't think I will ever be ready until I actually start putting one foot in front of the other.

Pre-Hikes

November 2001-March 2002

HARPERS FERRY, WEST VIRGINIA

My sister and I did our first overnight hike with a twenty-five-pound pack to test our new gear. I was surprised at how comfortable my pack felt. I don't think I will have a problem carrying more weight. We will add another fifteen to twenty pounds for our next outing.

We began our hike in Harpers Ferry, West Virginia. We thought we were going north only to find out an hour later that we were going south. It was an easy hike except for the climb out of town. I think every town has a climb in and out of it.

The David Lesser Shelter was full tonight. There was a group of Boy Scouts, a dad with his two sons, a couple on their third-month anniversary, and a few other weekend hikers camping at the shelter tonight. I was glad we brought our tents along. After we set up our tents and completed all our camp chores, we joined the others at the shelter. The data book said the water was a short distance downhill. It felt more like half a mile and straight down. Someone had opened some wine and invited us to join in. LaTripper had several glasses of wine and had a great time playing cards and drinking. I decided not to drink since I was hiking tomorrow.

The Appalachian Trail Conservancy at Harpers Ferry, West Virginia, stays open all winter, thanks to the hard work of some dedicated volunteers.

Winter of 2009 at Harpers Ferry, West Virginia

I see my path, but I don't know where it leads. Not knowing where I'm going is what inspires me to travel it.

Rosalia de Castro

PINE GROVE FURNACE, PENNSYLVANIA

LaTripper and I left from Pine Grove Furnace State Park, at mile marker 1090.3, on a cold rainy morning.

Pine Grove Furnace State Park, Pennsylvania

The furnaces were used to smelt iron during the Revolutionary and Civil Wars. The park has a campground with tent sites, public telephones, and a concession stand. Shortly north on the trail, you will pass Fuller Lake with a nice sand beach, where you can go swimming. The Ironmaster's Hostel is nearby.

By the time we drove there, it was twelve noon. This section of the trail is an easy hike and very well-maintained. It was exciting to see the official midpoint marker.

We had rain the entire day. It was colder than we expected, and we did not have any gloves with us, so we took our extra socks and wore them for gloves.

My sister slipped on the wet leaves and sprained her ankle quite badly. She didn't let me know how bad she was hurting until the next day.

Our goal was to stop at the James Frye shelter, better known as the Tagg Run shelter, for the night. We knew we were close, but with the rain, fog, and darkness setting in, we decided to set up our tents in the dark. Sis had a new tent and hadn't had a chance to practice setting it up yet. She was getting frustrated so I helped her set up hers before I began setting up mine. It was an extremely wet night, but my gear worked wonderfully. The next morning, we decided to hike a bit farther north to see how close we were to the shelter. If it had been daylight, we could have seen the access trail from where we stopped for the night.

LaTripper and Trapper Lee at the halfway marker just outside of Pine Grove, Pennsylvania

This was good practice for us, if nothing else. We continued to the shelter for a warm breakfast before heading south again and home. The spring at the shelter was dry so we went a bit farther north, where the data book indicated a stream for us to filter water from.

LaTripper has restless legs syndrome and was awake most of the night. She insisted she did not need a sleeping mat, which was part of the reason she was so cold. She told me the next morning that she was close to climbing into my tent with me. Imagine this in a single-man tent with barely enough room for one. She had decided to get a larger tent and a mat for the big hike. Every time we go out, we pick up a few new tips that will help us to be successful in completing our long hike.

CALEDONIA STATE PARK, PENNSYLVANIA

It seems that every time we go out, we are tested for every possible situation we might encounter when we actually start our long hike.

We had a nice hike in from the Caledonia State Park, Pennsylvania, and decided to head north on the trail. It was easy hiking today. My pack feels good.

Tumbling Run Shelter was very busy tonight so we decided to set our tents up a little north of the shelter. After setting up camp, we hiked north for about an hour and then came back to camp. We had a very enjoyable evening, sitting around the fire with the other hikers. We retired about 9:00 p.m. The rain, wind, and lightning began around 11:00 p.m. We found out the next morning that lightning had hit a tree by the shelter. I'm glad we decided to set up north of the shelter.

After the storm, the temperature dropped fast. We figured it was about twenty-five degrees by the next morning. We had ice on our tents, and our water bottles were frozen. Sis was tempted to crawl into my tent with me, which would have been a funny sight since I only have a one-man tent. I think we were finally ready.

Caledonia State Park is located in Adams and Franklin counties, midway between Chambersburg and

Gettysburg on US 30. Caledonia includes 1,125 acres of hiking, fishing, and camping activities. The park is in the northernmost section of the Blue Ridge Mountains known locally as South Mountain. Blue Mountain, the easternmost ridge of the Allegheny Mountains, is to the west and northwest of the park across a large, low, rolling, fertile valley known as the Great Valley. South Mountain is mostly composed of a hard rock called quartzite. The valleys on either side are underlined with limestone and shale. The soil is ideal for fruit production, proven by the abundance of orchards in the surrounding area.

Plumorchard Shelter

Daily Journal Entries

My journey will be the beginning of a new life for me. Things will never be as they were before. Being a woman on the Trail today will allow me to take the steps toward making dreams real.

This is a journal of my time on the Appalachian Trail. It includes some background information and history about various sections of the trail.

Resources for being a successful hiker or backpacker are also included throughout the book.

I don't claim to be a writer, just a dreamer who is living out her dreams.

GEORGIA

March 26-April 6, 2002

There are seventy-five miles of trail in Georgia, and the state flower is the Cherokee rose.

We left on Tuesday, the twenty-sixth of March, to head for Georgia, from Maryland.

Ed drove my sister Lorelei, my nephew Jason Snyder, and me to Georgia. Jason only has three months off from school so he is hiking as far as he can go. He only plans on eating trail mix to avoid going into town every few days, so he became known as "Gorp" along the trail

We all took turns driving the eleven hours it took us to reach Ellijay, Georgia. LaTripper and Jason got a hotel while Ed and I stayed in the van.

The next entry will be the first day on the Appalachian Trail.

Wednesday-Here we are! My journey is about to begin.

Most hikers who are starting their long journey from Georgia to Maine will begin at Amicalola Falls State Park. The name Amicalola in Cherokee means "tumbling waters."

From the park, you hike straight up to Amicalola Falls. The falls are worth seeing, but the extra miles are not part of the AT. The falls, at 729 feet high, are the tallest east of the Mississippi River. From there, you can climb to the top of Springer Mountain, which is a total of five and a half miles from the parking lot at USFS Road 28, and back down to the parking lot before heading north on the trail.

Down the Appalachian Trail, I could make out the first white paint blazes of the trail. I suddenly began to feel the excitement of getting underway.

The trail from the parking lot to the top of Springer Mountain climbs constantly but never sharply. The ground is rocky and a bit slippery with the ice. The GATC has added a few steps in a couple of places and a unique water control network. Partway up to the summit, there were views looking down into the Cartecay River watershed. The view only got better as we approached the summit. All the trees were covered with ice. The rush I experienced being there was indescribable. Coming back down the mountain, the ice started melting and falling. It was like walking through an ice storm.

The hardest part was saying good bye to Ed. I will miss him very much. However, I will carry him close to my heart during my hike.

We stayed in our tents at Hawk Mountain Shelter. The shelter was full. For our first night, we had a full moon with clear skies and lots of stars. My gear worked wonderfully.

Thursday-It was a very challenging day with many climbs. We climbed three mountains up to an elevation of 3,500 feet. It was a very sunny day with a high of sixty degrees. We did well, considering how out of shape we are. The country is so pretty. At times, we were walking through canopies of rhododendrons, the next few miles; we were at the summit of a mountain with scenic views.

We are already ahead of schedule so we will probably do a five- or six-mile day tomorrow. Blood Mountain is ahead so we will pace ourselves. The people on the trail are great! There are parents, out for a few days with their son, hiking a small section of the trail. We have been labeled "the sisters" in the camp registers. Each shelter has a register where the hikers enter notes of encouragement or maybe a message for a co-hiker. It's great fun to read the entries. My nephew Jason is not hiking with us. There is an entry in the book from him stating he did sixteen miles the first day.

A typical day at camp is getting to the shelter, getting water for the night and breakfast, washing up, cooking, and building a fire, if any wood is available. We are all sitting around the campfire tonight and sharing day number two's adventures.

We stopped at Gooch Gap Shelter for the night. We completed 7.3 miles today.

Friday-We were seeing so many beautiful wildflowers. I was learning their names as I went. I wish I had brought my wildflower book with me.

Today was very strenuous for me. Sis kept me going, though. We stopped at Woody Gap for lunch, where the trail intersects GA Route 60 near Suches, Georgia.

There are picnic tables, a privy, and a spring just a short walk up a side trail.

We met Jabazz, a thru-hiker from 2001, who was out for a few days, chatting with all the hikers and just enjoying being back out on the trail again.

Duct tape is a wonder fix for everything. I had both big toes taped. I started to get a blister, and I think the tape has taken care of the problem. We are eating well and finding plenty of water so far.

We are making so many trail friends. Flat Lander and In Your Dreams, a father-and-son team, dropped off the trail today. They hitched a ride to Neel's Gap. They were having problems with their feet, and their packs were too heavy. They are skipping Blood Mountain and will hop on beyond that.

I'm writing this entry in the dark, sitting on top of the mountain, overlooking the town below. We are at the most beautiful bluff tonight. Before dark, the view was of the chain of mountains with no indication of a town until dark. All of a sudden, all the lights of the town started coming on as if by magic, and it appeared as if the sky was full of fireflies.

There is rain with thunderstorms forecast for tonight and more rain for the next few days. I'm not happy about that.

Amy and Shawn, a husband and wife, showed up just before dark. We had hiked on and off with them for the last few days, and we were happy to see them. Shortly afterward, Flat Lander and In Your Dreams showed up. It was tight, but it was nice to have company in such a remote area, knowing we were in for a night of thunderstorms. The wind, rain, and lightning began about 11:00 p.m., and it poured all night. My gear worked well. Everything was dry inside even though I was sitting in the middle of a mud hole by morning.

We stopped at the top of Big Cedar Mountain and completed six miles today.

Saturday -We packed our tent and gear up in the rain this morning.

Today, we hiked from Big Cedar Mountain to Woods Hole Shelter in the rain. It never stopped all day. It seems like we climbed all day up to an elevation of 3,740 feet and back down again to about 3,000 feet in a matter of two miles. From there, we climbed the rest of the day up to 3,590 feet in the rain. Our packs were heavy with our wet gear, and I was never so happy to see a shelter. Now that is a whole different story. Everyone else had the same idea—to get warm and dry as quickly as possible. The shelter was designed to sleep seven people, and we had at least twenty-five hikers show up. Nine set up on the platform, and we decided to move the picnic table outside so another seven hikers could sleep on the gravel. They were under the roof, but I'm sure the gravel was not very comfortable. I set up along the feet of the other hikers on the platform. There were four tents set up; my sister's being one of them. I was worried about my sister when the lightning started. She told me the next morning she was scared when there was a really bad crash of lightning. It rained all night, but I was lucky to have stayed warm and safe.

I'm having some problems with the altitude, but each day, it seems to be getting easier.

We completed 5.9 miles today.

Sunday-We were on the trail by 8:00 a.m. We wanted to get to Neel's Gap and over Blood Mountain before the rain starts again.

We ate as we walked to save some time. I was nervous about climbing Blood Mountain even though it wasn't that bad. The descent was even worse. We started at 3,590 feet and went up to 4,450 feet in less than two miles. We then went down to 3,200 feet. I would like to go back to Blood Mountain in the future and explore it further. We were fogged in and could not see the views. There is an old stone shelter with a fireplace at the top of the mountain. Not many hikers stay here since it is infested with mice and is said to be very damp and cold.

When we were close to Neel's Gap, which was on our first night in town, the only thing we could think of was a stack of pancakes, but there was none to be found. We decided to stay in a cabin instead of go to the hostel as planned. We all agreed we would not be affording this luxury very often. Another girl, Jean "Jagg," shared the cabin with us. She left today, but we stayed an extra day. We are going to shop for four days of food, which will hold us until our next mail drop. We are also mailing some things home.

Our town box arrived in time. It was nice to have a hot shower with real shampoo. We shuttled to town for dinner. The van was free for thru-hikers so we all sat together at dinner. We are in a dry county, so no beer. We took Monday off.

We stopped at Neel's Gap and only hiked 3.7 miles today.

> Blood Mountain is the sixth highest mountain, rising to 4,450 feet. Legends have it that the mountain got its name from the bloody battles fought here by the Creek and Cherokee Indians. The mountain is the most visited spot on the Trail south of Clingman's Dome. The impact of more than forty thousand visitors a year has taken its toll on this sensitive terrain.

Tuesday-It got up to eighty degrees today. We're starting to pick up the pace now. I'm doing better with the altitude. The highest elevation was 3,800 feet. We keep making a new group of friends. We hike together for a few days, and then they either hike ahead or drop off for a few days. I had to buy a new sleeping bag. The Slumberjack™

bag blew out at the feet. My sisters did the same. The shelter is full tonight. It's calling for rain again. Hope to get an early start.

We stopped at Low Gap Shelter and hiked 10.4 miles today.

Wednesday-This shelter is known for the cold north winds blowing up from the gap below.

It was uphill most of the day. Our speed is getting better. We went from 3,000 feet to 3,700 feet. It was an easy walk from there for the next four and a half miles. The climb up Blue Mountain was very hard, with lots of rocks to contend with. I guess it's just a sample of what is ahead of us. We've been hiking with Buzz today. Ed will appreciate her trail name. She got her name because she buzzed her head before hitting the trail. Ed had tried to get me to do the same, but I lost my nerve.

This shelter has food-hoist cables for bear protection. We have a very rough day tomorrow with a very steep climb down and then back up again.

We made it as far as Blue Mountain Shelter, which is 7.2 miles from Low Gap Shelter.

Thursday-We had the most incredible sunrise this morning. That's what being out here is all about. I was able to view the sunrise from my sleeping bag. It was very cold last night. It probably got down to the low thirties.

We went from 3,970 feet down to 2,950 feet the first thing in the morning. Next, we're climbing again up to 3,970 feet up to Rocky Mountain. It was beautiful, but every mountain I come to is even more breathtaking than the last. We continued to climb up to Tray Mountain, which is 4,430 feet to the summit. Good spot to view the Canada warbler. Males are blue gray with a yellow chest. They appear to have a necklace around their neck. These are such beautiful songbirds so take time for a nice break here.

The evening view was of the mountain range with the lights of the town below. Today, the weather was perfect. No rain! We met a group of women out hiking for two weeks. They said they would follow us on TrailJournals.com. One of the ladies recognized us from our trail journals and said she had been following our preparation stage. We met another family that wanted to follow us out for a day. They gave us some trail mix they had left over.

My health is good, my feet are doing okay, and my pack feels good. Each day is a new experience. I still love being out here. I'm not having the old neck pain, but my right knee is quite swollen.

We only have nineteen more miles before we reach North Carolina. We're seeing a lot of fire damage from a few weeks ago. We stopped at Tray Mountain Shelter and hiked a total of 7.7 miles.

Friday-We left camp with a nice cool breeze and the sun shining. This was the hardest day yet. I'm getting better on the climbs though. The climb up Kelly Knob was very hard for me. It was straight up with no switchbacks. We went straight up from 3,300 feet to 4,250 feet.

We passed the Deep Gap Shelter and decided to push onward to the Blueberry Patch Hostel for the night.

We hitchhiked three and a half miles on US 76 west at Dicks Creek Gap, Hiawassee to The Blueberry Patch hostel. A young salesman stopped and gave us a ride. When we arrived, last in as usual, we found the bunkhouse already full. They only allow so many tents in the backyard, and that was also full to its maximum. My sister was so tired she announced "I don't care; I am going to put my tent up in the yard." Our gracious hosts agreed to allow two more tents for the night.

The hostel is an organic blueberry farm owned by 1991 thru-hiker Gary Potent and his wife Lennie. They have a shower house, laundry, and shuttle service back to the trail. We went to town for pizza and beer and sat with Frank, Robin Hood, and Tellger. This was a wonderful change from trail food. Most hikers go through their mailbox and sort what they need and leave what they don't in a box that is left for unwanted items. If you come up short on supplies at any given time, you may help yourself from this box.

I talked to Eddie tonight. It's always so good to hear his voice. I miss him more than I can say. I felt bad for LaTripper. I found her crying in her tent. She was feeling very homesick.

We completed 10.6 miles today.

Saturday-Lennie prepared coffee, orange juice, and blueberry pancakes. The nicest part was sharing the feast at their dining room table with them.

We took the shuttle back to the trail and planned to do a short day today. When we got back to Dick's Creek Gap, there was a man with candy bars and soda for the hikers. It was such a treat to have so many goodies since our supply gets so boring at times. Dr. Paul S. was also giving out soda, fruit, vegetables, etc. They are who we call trail angels out here. The support and encouragement from the community are quite special. It really keeps your spirits up.

My feet are tender but not blistered. I talk a lot about my feet, but that is the most important health issue out here. It means going on or going home. My knee is swollen and painful today. I'm looking for a stick to help with the one hiking pole I have. I will get a second one when we get to town. We hiked most of the day with our new friend Buzz. She is our age and lots of fun to be with. Veggie also has a knee problem, and he has slowed down to our speed, which is usually slower than most. Our buddy Frank also hiked on and off with us today. It's nice how everyone takes care of each other out here. You're never really alone.

We have a lot of climbing tomorrow. I don't think I want to set up a tent tonight.

The Plumorchard Gap Shelter was airlifted in, fully assembled. This is the nicest shelter we have stayed in so far.

We only completed 4.3 miles of the trail today.

NORTH CAROLINA AND TENNESSEE

April 7-May 14, 2002

There are 371 miles of trail in North Carolina and Tennessee. The state flower for North Carolina is the dogwood, for Tennessee, it's the iris.

Sunday is another day of climbing. After numerous ups and downs, we finally made it to the North Carolina line. I was getting very discouraged just short of the border. As usual, I was in the rear, coming up slow. Buzz, Amy, Shawn, and my sister were waiting at the border for me. I broke down crying just a few meters short and said, "I can't go any further." The team cheered me in, and we had quite a joyous celebration to have completed our first state.

Kim "Sketcher" Sevy and Susan "Sherpa Mom" Settle—Cheoah Bald, North Carolina

When we arrived at camp, everyone agreed that it was one of the hardest hikes so far. I found a stick to assist me. It did make a big difference. Camp is always fun. We are still with the same group; they just always get to camp sooner than we do. It's cold tonight—in the twenties. Tomorrow, we plan to do either five or twelve and a half miles. If it's still cold in the morning, we will leave late and take a short day. Our highest elevation climb tomorrow is 4,760 feet. We completed 7.3 miles and decided to stop at the Muskrat Creek Shelter for the night. This shelter sits high at 4,600 feet.

Tree at Georgia and North Carolina state line— Bly Gap

It is not so much for its beauty that the forest makes a claim upon men's hearts, as for that subtle something, that quality of air that emanation from old trees, that so wonderfully changes and renews a weary spirit.

Robert Louis Stevenson

Monday-We hiked along the blue-blazed Kimsey Creek Trail instead of taking the AT over Standing Indian Mountain. We missed twelve miles of the AT by taking this alternate route. I would like to have seen Standing Indian Mountain, but we weren't up to a 5,498-foot climb.

Cherokee legend has it that a great winged monster once inhabited the mountain, and during the monster's reign, warriors were posted on the mountain as lookouts. As the story goes, a tremendous bolt of lightning shattered the mountain and killed the monster. During the strike, a lone Cherokee sentinel was hit by the bolt and turned into stone, supposedly for being a poor sentry.

It was a gentle hike through the valley. We walked along the stream for most of the hike. Everything was so green and lush. We hiked all day with Amy, Shawn, Buzz, and Brian. They carried a cell phone with them and were able to call ahead to see if there was any vacancy at the Rainbow Springs Campground. This campground is an old US 64, about ten miles from Franklin, North Carolina. We enjoyed catching up with Brian, Ramblin Man, Eric, and Crispy.

We stayed at the Rainbow Springs Campground and completed twelve miles today.

Tuesday-We took another day off and stayed at the campground. It was so nice to sleep in and have no agendas today. We had pizza for dinner and ice cream for dessert, of course. Wow, what a treat.

Amy and Shawn left this morning. I hope we can catch up with them again. Both of them are entertainers from Nashville. Her genre is bluegrass. We were unable to convince them to sing for us. Buzz and Frank stayed over and will leave with us tomorrow. We seem to be losing the group of hikers we started with. LaTripper and I have always hiked our hike instead of raced to reach the finish line by a designated date. If we get there, great, if not, we gave it our best shot.

I found this ditty written in the register at one of the shelters:

That Smell in the Shelter

Poly-pro socks after five days of wearing
Will have the hardiest hikers a swearing
Boots made of Gore-Tex® they never will dry.
Armpit alarms that will just make you cry.
Synthetic fibers, an odor they hold.
After three months of hiking, your boots start to mold.
Ninety degrees with the heat and the sweat,
Or after the rain when the shelter is wet,
When you finally get in at the end of the day,
And you're ready to rest, anyhow, anyway,
It's that smell in the shelter, so let's give it a yell.
So hooray for that odor, nose-quivering tingle
I know it's disgusting
But I hope you like my jingle.

Author Unknown

Wednesday-We had a near-perfect day today. Our ascents and descents were much more moderate, and I did much better today. I think a day off works miracles. I had some lessons on proper pole use along with tips for controlling your breathing.

We made good time today. We did 7.3 miles in a little more than five hours. I saw the most beautiful waterfall at Winding Stair Gap. Sure wish I had my camera.

I've been seeing a lot of grouse today. Sometimes, we would be walking along, and all of a sudden one would flush out of the bushes, scaring us half to death. The birds are also getting more active. It is so nice to hear them singing all day long. This is one of the reasons I don't hike with a radio. I would miss all the beautiful sights and sounds. The trees are beginning to bud out. All is well with the world and me. I'm so happy and content with life, except for missing Eddie. We have now completed 110.5 miles. I didn't think I would ever see the day I could hike more than one hundred miles.

Siler Bald Shelter has food hoists also. I think the rest of North Carolina will be taking precautions with any bears that might smell all that trail mix we eat. While in bear country, it is recommended that you don't sleep in the clothes that you hike or cook in. Also, include your toothpaste and any items with fragrance in the food bag when you hang it up. Looks like a girls' night at the shelter tonight. We have Buzz, Grayson, LaTripper, and me.

We completed 7.3 miles today.

Thursday-It is an absolutely perfect day. It was misty and cool until about 1:00 p.m. Again, we have the most incredible views. I'm enjoying North Carolina more than Georgia since we have some easy terrain in between climbs. I'm gaining speed and endurance on the uphill climbs now. We climbed up to 5,340 feet, and I seem to have gotten over my altitude problems. My breathing is more regulated, and I'm not getting headaches anymore. The hike from Wayah Gap up to Wayah Bald was absolutely breathtaking. There is a stone observation tower at the top, which offers views of the meandering mountain ranges.

We had lunch on top of the mountain. The last three days have been absolutely perfect! I wish I could bottle the spring water we are drinking. It is some of the best. It runs right by the shelter, which is nice.

We hiked 12.1 miles today. Cold Spring Shelter is a bad shelter! There are lots of mice. Next time, I will stay in my tent. The Civilian Conservation Corps (CCC) built this shelter in 1933, and it shows.

Here is some advice for anyone who might be planning a long-distance hike on the AT: Don't get discouraged in Georgia! Georgia is known for its PUDs (pointless ups and downs). You are going either up or down, with no relief in between. If you make it to North Carolina, you will be in peak shape and able to enjoy one of the most beautiful countries in the world.

Friday-We started out at 5,200 feet this morning and went down to 4,700 feet. From there, we descended to 1,800 feet in approximately six miles into the Nantahala Gorge.

The constant descent is very hard on the feet and knees. There are quite a few hikers who drop off here since the descent can cause severe injuries to the knees. Go slow, and wear a knee brace especially if you have any problems to start with. I had to wait for LaTripper at the bottom for about twenty minutes. She is not good on descents. She has a fear of falling. Even though it was a challenging hike down, we did have some breathtaking views.

At the bottom, you cross US 19. From US 19, the trail passes through the Nantahala Outdoor Center. This is a great spot to take a break and go whitewater rafting or kayaking.

We had a mail drop to pick up here. At first, it could not be found, but the next day, they eventually found it. Before they located our box, everyone took pity on us and gave us enough food to hold us to Fontana Dam, where we could replenish our supplies. From here, you cross over the Nantahala River, where you can watch the whitewater rafting from a pedestrian bridge and go up to the hikers' hostel from there.

I was very tired tonight. LaTripper and I have a room with a real bed, if you want to call it that. It's just a wood bunk, and you put your pad and sleeping bag on this platform.

I will be mailing some things home that I'm not using or will not need since the weather is getting warmer.

The trees in the lower elevations are really budding out. We saw lots of wildlife today. We hiked 11.5 miles today.

Nantahala, in Cherokee, means "River of the noonday Sun." The gorge is so steep it only gets sun for a very short time at noon each day.

Saturday-We didn't hike many miles today, but the climb out of the gorge was straight up. This gorge has the steepest ascent and descent of any gorge on the entire trail. This has to be one of my hardest days yet, but I did it. I think I was getting overheated. Thank goodness it started raining, and it cooled me off. These days of accomplishment are what I'm out here for. It is making me a stronger person in more ways than just physical strength. We made it in just slightly more than five hours. Everyone cheered us when we arrived at the shelter.

I was very nervous on the ridge when it started raining, and we had to scramble through some very slippery rocks. When it began to thunder, we really became concerned since we were at the summit at that time. There was nowhere to go but continue up and over. I can't believe how strong my lungs and legs are getting on these climbs.

I saw a four-foot black snake in the middle of the trail today. I just nudged him with my pole and continued up the trail.

The wildflowers are beautiful. We have seen various colors of trillium, bluetts, pink lady slippers, and spring beauty.

We have now completed 141 miles. The shelter was full tonight, so we put up our tents. I love my tent. It offers me my private space, and I sleep so much better. Stayed dry in the rain, but I hate packing up a wet tent since it adds weight to your pack.

I'm getting used to eating oatmeal since it is something I never eat at home. I just add lots of brown sugar, raisins, cinnamon, and powdered milk. I have been eating well, my spirits are good, and I still love being out here even though we have a few really rough days.

I bought another hiking pole to match the one I already had. What a difference it made on my knee. I used it coming up out of the gorge. I don't think I would have made it up without it. I also bought another sleeping bag that adds ten degrees for the cold nights in the Smoky Mountains. I sent the other one home.

After completing 6.9 miles, we stopped at the Sassafras Gap Shelter for the night.

When the data book says the shelter has a privy, it means an outhouse—usually without a door, down the hill, and smelly.

I really miss Eddie and talking to all my children. I have not been able to get on a computer to check my e-mail.

Sunday-It rained on and off all day, but I enjoyed the cooler temperatures. As soon as we left camp, we began to climb up to 5,200 feet to the summit of Cheoah Bald. I heard the views were fabulous, but we were fogged in by the time we reached the top. From there, we descended into Stecoah Gap. We were so delighted to see a Trail Angel handing out sodas. What a treat to have something other than water to drink. I guess he knew that we were about to climb again. From there, it was straight up again, with a one-thousand-foot gain. This has been said to be the steepest climb in the south.

I saw another snake today.

The shelter is full again tonight. The shelters have not been as nice as the ones in Georgia. We will probably do a short day tomorrow and leave late in the morning. There are not as many climbs either. It should be an easier day for us. Each night, before we retire, my sister and I go over the maps and the data books and plan our next day.

We stopped at the Brown Fork Gap Shelter after completing 9.1 miles today.

Monday-Today was one of our best days. There was only one uphill climb, and the rest of the day was just rolling country with a few downhill hikes. Grayson caught up with us and will be hiking with us again.

Chilly Willy and Just Ray were at the shelter when we arrived. When we decided to stop for the night, it was LaTripper, Grayson, Chilly Willy, Just Ray, and me. When we finally settled in for the night, we got the giggles, and this went on for a good half hour. We tried to be quiet since Chilly Willy and Just Ray were already sleeping. They told us they never heard a word.

Buzz and Frank are ahead of us now. I hope we can catch up with them. We miss their humor, and they were always our cheering committee when we roll into camp, last of course.

I had my first real fall today. I was very lucky that I was not injured since I slipped while climbing down a steep rock. When I stopped, I was straddling a very jagged rock.

I was beating myself up today. I'm still struggling on the really steep ascents, but today, I felt like a twenty-year-old. We were on a steep three-mile downhill. At the bottom, I had two twenty-year-olds tell me they could not keep up with me. I needed that boost of encouragement.

LaTripper is doing well. We have been sharing proper techniques in using our poles. We don't always see eye to eye on things, but overall, we get along nicely. She informed me that I was mothering her too much and wanted me to back off. I agreed, but I guess being a mother to three children will do that to you. I love her and felt I needed to be aware of her safety since she is seven years younger.

We were the first to arrive at the shelter tonight. It was nice to arrive early and just relax. Usually, when we get to camp, we start by setting up our tents or space in the shelter, find a tree to hang our food, get enough water for the night and morning, cook supper, clean up, and get ready for bed.

We went as far as Cable Gap Shelter and completed 6.1 miles today.

Tuesday-It was a nice hike to Fontana Dam. I love the white trout lilies in this area.

We decided not to stay at the Fontana Hilton Hostel. The Fontana Dam Visitor Center has a small store that sells sodas and snacks and has free showers. You can get your park self-registration permit here if they are open. We were disappointed to find everything closed since we were hoping to get a good lunch at the visitor's center

We called the Hike Inn and were able to get a room. They said they would pick us up, but it would be an hour before they could get there. While we were waiting, a man who said he had been hiking approached us and asked us if we needed a ride. It appeared he had been living out of his car. We thanked him for the offer but informed him we had a ride coming. He shared some of his energy bars with us and told us he was not going out on the trail for the time being.

We found the Hike Inn to be very friendly to hikers. Jeff and Nancy Hoch own it. After we cleaned up, we caught a shuttle, along with other hikers, to Robbinsville, North Carolina. We had a good dinner with all the other hikers, took care of our laundry, and did some shopping before catching the shuttle back to the inn. I had a much-needed restful night. We only hiked 5.5 miles today.

If the national terrorism alert level is high (red), public facilities at the dam will close, and hikers must follow a blue-blazed route over the Little Tennessee River below the dam.

Fontana Dam, NC is 480 feet high. It is the highest dam in the eastern United States. The dam is the southern boundary of the Great Smoky Mountains National Park.

GREAT SMOKY MOUNTAINS NATIONAL PARK

Wednesday-Once we cross over the dam, we will take a right and enter into the Great Smoky Mountains National Park. The park straddles the border between North Carolina and Tennessee. I have been waiting for this the entire hike. I'm so excited about being in the Smoky Mountains.

It was a long climb from Fontana Dam to Shuckstack Mountain, where the fire tower is located. We did not take the short detour to climb the tower. The Benton MacKaye Trail intersects with the Appalachian Trail at Sassafras Gap and at Davenport Gap. Birch Spring Gap has campsites and tent pads, but we decided to continue on for a few more miles.

It started out quite hot but cooled off as the clouds came in. I saw our first deer today. She was standing right in the middle of the trail.

The wildflowers are extraordinary. A soft filigree of flowering dogwood dappled the valley as we passed through it. It is so peaceful and serene here.

If you don't mind the extra weight, I recommend carrying a flower and a bird book to identify each as you hike along.

We hiked with Grayson today. Buzz is still one day ahead of us, and Frank showed up late at the shelter.

This is my first night in the park. I'm getting nervous because of all the bear warnings posted along the trail. When we got to the shelter, we found a chain fence on the front of the shelter. Most of the shelters in the Smokies have fireplaces in them to enjoy, if you are lucky enough to find and dry wood to burn. One of my biggest concerns, when I decided to do a thru-hike, was the bear. But I know my determination and courage will get me through my fears.

The bugs are really bad tonight. I hope the campfire helps. We had the most beautiful sunset tonight.

I guess we have beaten the odds. At Fontana Dam, the statistics show that at least two-thirds of thru-hikers will drop off at this point of their hike. We are still in the one-third of remaining hikers attempting to hike the entire trail.

We stayed at Mollies Ridge Shelter and completed 12.4 miles.

The park was established in 1934. The Smoky Mountain National Park is the most visited of the traditional national parks. For this reason, it is especially important to practice the Leave No Trace policy in this area. The highest elevation on the AT is found here at Clingman's Dome, at 6,643 feet. The park also has the most rainfall and snowfall in the South, and many hikers are caught off guard by the snow and cold temperatures. You should avoid sending cold-weather gear home until you complete this section through the park.

The Trail through the park is home to the most diverse forest in North America. The park includes more than one hundred species of trees, 1,570 species of flowering plants, sixty species of mammals, more than twenty-five different salamanders, and 2,000 varieties of mushrooms.

Permits are required and can be obtained at the self-registration facility near the pay phone at the dam's visitor's center. Violators can be fined $125.

There are between four hundred and six hundred bears in the park. They become more active in the spring and remain active through fall. Over the years, they have developed a taste for the food humans carry. Be sure to hang your food along with any items with fragrance (toothpaste, etc.).

Prepare your food away from your sleeping area, and don't sleep in the clothes you have cooked in.

Most shelters in the park have bear chain-link fencing across the front. Mollies Ridge Shelter was built in 1961 and was renovated in 2003. The fencing has been removed, and a covered porch has been added, with benches.

The SMHC and the ATC are rebuilding or replacing all the shelters in the park. All the rebuilt shelters will have the chain-link fencing removed. They all have food hoists, so you don't have to go looking for a tree to hang your food. Tenting is not allowed, and if you are section-hiking, you need to reserve a spot in the shelters.[2]

Thursday-We climbed Rocky Top, Thunderhead, Brier Knob, and Chestnut Bald. The highest climb was up to the summit of Thunderhead at an elevation of 5,527 feet. We had an extraordinary view at the top of Thunderhead.

When you are in the park, you follow the ridges most of the day. Some of the most magnificent views can be found along these ridges in the Great Smoky Mountains National Park GSMNP. If you look to the right, you see the Blue Ridge Mountain range in North Carolina, and if you look left, you see the Tennessee range. These mountains are often known as the Gentle Mountains.

It was a very long day for us even though we only did 11.7 miles. Hopefully, we will take a shorter day tomorrow. The bugs are quite bad today. I had to use my bug net over my head when we would take a break. They don't bother you as much if you keep moving. It's been in the eighties for the last three days now. It started raining about one hour before reaching camp. That helped to cool things down and get rid of the pesky bugs.

It was not a fabulous day for me. I think I pushed myself too hard today. All I need is a restful night of sleep, and I will be as good as new in the morning. I'm missing Eddie and family today. I will see Eddie in about one week. This will be the longest time without a town day since we started. It's about seventy-one miles to get through the park. It will take us about seven days since we don't push the miles. We are trying to enjoy each and every view, which are many.

I had hoped to sleep in the shelter tonight, but it was full when we arrived. Well, LaTripper took care of me, knowing I was exhausted and nervous about sleeping in my tent with bears in the area. She helped me set up my tent and kept reassuring me that all would be okay if I followed all the rules. It's nice to have her to lean on when I've had a down day. My sister and I are usually aware of the needs of each other. That seems to make us very compatible while hiking every day.

Just as we finished setting up, a thunderstorm, with strong winds and hail, started blowing. It was blowing so hard that I was

---

Appalachian Trail Thru-Hikers Companion, 2007 Edition[2]

concerned about my tent blowing away. I was happy to find everything was dry. I had a very restless night since all I could think of was a bear sneaking into camp. If I'm going to make it the rest of the way, I need to overcome this fear.

We stopped at Derrick Knob Shelter and completed 11.7 miles today.

Friday-Well obviously, the bears didn't eat me last night. I have another night under my belt so I guess it will get easier each night. It was an easier day today. It was sunny and much cooler today. We're starting to go through pine forest now. It's a nice change from the open terrain. We had a deer in camp this morning. I've been hearing grouse all day now. We stopped at Silers Bald Shelter for lunch and then we pushed on. While we were filtering water at the spring, we had a fabulous view of the Blue Ridge Mountains, its one range after another that never seems to end. We hung up our wet gear to dry while we had lunch.

We got to the top of a bald, and the AT sign showed a split in two different directions, or so we thought. So LaTripper said, "You go right, and I'll go left." So off we went. I kept hiking for some time and started to get concerned when she didn't show up. I asked several hikers if they knew about the split in the trail a short distance south of here. They had no idea what I was talking about. I told them I thought I had lost my sister, and I identified her. I asked them if they saw her to let her know I would be waiting for her at the next shelter. After a while, I met a ranger, and I shared the same story with her. The ranger said the trail did not split and that the trail to the left was only a trail to a viewpoint. It did not connect to the AT. I really became concerned at this time. I again identified my sister and left the same message for her where she could catch up with me. I decided to wait on a log for her to catch up. Finally, I saw Sis coming up the trail.

She had tried going down from the overlook before she realized it was a mistake and backtracked to the trail. I'm so thankful it all worked out.

The flowers are still abundant and very beautiful. There are sections where the entire forest floor is covered with flowers called spring beauty. From a distance, you would think the forest floor is covered with snow.

I'm always hungry now. I can't seem to get enough to eat. I got sunburned today. I forgot to put sunscreen on.

I had a perfect day today. It was much better than yesterday. The day got even better when Banjo showed up. He pulled out his banjo and began to sing and play bluegrass for all of us. I just felt like getting up and doing a little clogging. That would have been quite a sight in my camp sandals.

We have a full shelter again tonight. There are a lot of weekend hikers out today. Okay with that tonight. My tent is so cozy and safe.

Our shelter for tonight is Double Spring Gap Shelter. We hiked 7.2 miles today.

Saturday-Today was an absolutely perfect day. We hiked the most miles in one day so far. Today, we climbed the highest mountain on the trail at 6,643 feet. Today, we climbed Clingman's Dome. There is an observation tower that provides a 360-degree view. We did not go up to the tower, however. The summit is usually busy since there is an access road up to the top. Fraser firs and red spruce are now dying out in this section of the forest. It's so sad to see. The views were some of the best so far. It was much cooler today with a nice breeze all day. We walked most of the day in pine forests, which is always a welcome change. This is our fourth day in the park. We should make it through in three more days. I can't wait for a shower. We stopped for a break at Newfound Gap (US 441). We had a lady, whom we had met on the trail, who offered us a ride to Gatlinburg. We came so close to accepting, but declined. I kept hoping to see Eddie at the Gap but no luck. We had three more miles to the shelter, so we hit the trail. This section is very rocky with some climbs. Sis had fallen earlier, so we cleaned her abrasions in the restroom before we started out again.

I'm eating all day now. I hope my food lasts for three more days. Ice Water Spring Shelter is our home for the night. We completed 13.8 miles today.

Sunday-We walked along the ridge all day. We had mountain ranges on both sides. I felt like I was in heaven. We are having lunch on the summit of Laurel Top Mountain with the most gorgeous sight imaginable. I feel like I'm in God's country. My heart is soaring. I'm having trouble relating the feelings I have, which are so overwhelming at times. Sometimes, I feel like I'm going to burst with the excitement inside me. We had cool breezes all day again. It makes my hike more enjoyable. We have been at 5,500 to 6,000 feet all day. The altitude bothers me at times on the climbs but not like in Georgia. It's so peaceful up here. The birds have been singing to me the entire day. There are no bugs up here.

We did an assessment of our remaining food only to realize that we only had enough to get us through two more days. We have twenty-two more miles to go so we will try to split the difference in two days. We are looking forward to a place called Mountain Mama's for some good home-cooking and our next mail drop.

We hiked up Charlie's Bunion with views of Mount Le Conte to the west. This mountain got its name because the outcropping stuck out like a bunion on a foot.

Charlie's Bunion by Bruce Stansberry

We had one of the worst challenges today. We came to a landslide across the trail. We had to work our way down, across the bottom, and then up the other side. I went first, since my sister was scared, and said I would help pull her up from there. I had to throw my poles up and over, and then I began rock-climbing with forty-five pounds on my back.

It was quite nerve-wracking since the drop was off the side of the mountain if I slipped. I didn't let my sister know how scared I was, but I made it up okay. I then talked LaTripper up, but she was crying because she was so scared. I was so proud of her for pushing the rest of the way up the mountain. I picked her a bunch of wild violets to cheer her up.

All the trees are starting to bloom now. The forest is coming alive. I get so excited just being here and becoming part of nature and all its beauty.

We stopped at Peck's Corner Shelter and completed 7.4 miles today.

Monday-I woke up to rain this morning, but it stopped by the time we hit the trail. We had another great hiking day. It was easy terrain for the most part. It was in the forty- to sixty-degree range all day. That is the best temperature for hiking. We hiked almost thirteen miles in seven hours today.

We are running out of food and getting a bit concerned. Matt "Sky Blue Night" gave us tuna and pancake mix. We finally came down off the ridge after many descents. Tomorrow will be downhill most of the day as well.

In 1984, an F-4 Phantom fighter plane crashed into the ridge between Inadu Knob and Old Black. Some of the wreckage from this crash remains scattered about the area, with a number of fragments located in an area along the trail. We could see them from the trail and decided to hike down and check it out. When we got to camp, someone had carried a section of the wreckage into camp with them.

We are at camp tonight with a married couple, Frank, Poetry in Motion, Sky Blue Night, Possum, Beach, LaTripper and me. Everyone pushed ahead to Davenport and a town day. It is cool tonight. It got down to about thirty-five degrees. I crawled into my tent early. I will call Ed tomorrow and set a time and place for us to meet.

We camped at Cosby Knob Shelter after hiking 12.9 miles.

Tuesday-Today was great! As we were hiking, the wind was blowing flower petals from the trees, and it appeared as if it were snowing. The forest, in the lower elevations, is so alive now. Everything is getting green, flowers are all in bloom, and weather is gorgeous. We hiked the final eight miles of the Great Smoky Mountains National Park (GSMNP). From there, we continued on for another two-and-a-half-mile hike to the hostel in Davenport Gap, Tennessee. We stayed at Mountain Mama's Kuntry Store and Hostel. They charge $15.00 a night, and you get a towel, shower, laundry facility, and a shuttle back to the trail. The hostel is located on route 32 and NC 284.

Tuesday, April 23—my fifty-sixth birthday

Birthday

Birthdays, had so many, left with so few.
With my crazy life, what yet will I do?
Perhaps dance, till I wear out yet another pair of dancing shoes,
As I listen to those down and dirty blues.
Life is full of friends, foes, and strangers yet to meet.
Just a big people stew . . . so what will I do?
Spend my next birthday years traveling roads still unknown.
Wrapping music round me, thinking on how beautiful
These children of mine have grown.
Bringing up the memories stored away, of people I once have known.
They were here so short a time,
needed to go where their own wind does blow.
Tell me of the future, do you know what I have yet to do?
Perhaps wear leather, get a tattoo, and just be wild.
Spend too long so humble, being so old, just wishing to be a child.
What do I do? My years are so few.

Janeen Schneider, my sister

We got our mail drop on time. We also had a package from a lady we had met on the trail. She is a second grade teacher, and she had her class do pictures with a note from each of them. That was so special. It brought tears to my eyes, knowing that there are people who care about us being out here.

Wednesday-Coming out of the gap, we walked along the river for two miles. We saw several thundering waterfalls. The mountain laurel and dogwood are in full bloom now. Absolutely breathtaking! We continued climbing very steeply for the next six miles and crossed back into North Carolina.

As we came over the top of Snow Bird Mountain, we heard someone calling for help. A father and his daughter were coming up, but his daughter Trip was very ill. He was trying to catch a volunteer, who was working on the trail, in hopes of getting some help for his daughter. We sat with Trip, while her dad ran to catch the volunteer. They had carried cheeseburgers, which they had bought at Mountain Mama's, for six hours. After eating them, Trip was experiencing food poisoning.

The shelter is full again tonight so we are sleeping in our tents. We retired early since it was getting quite chilly.

We stayed at Groundhog Creek Shelter at Deep Gap and completed another 9.6 miles today.

Thursday-It stayed around forty degrees most of the morning. The sun finally came out, but we were still cold. I have never seen so many shades of trillium before. There are pink, white, maroon, and even yellow ones. I think my favorite is the maroon ones. The forest is covered with them. It's like walking on a continuous carpet of blooms. Today, I felt like I was walking on an aisle of flower petals as they kept falling from the trees above. I never knew there were so many varieties of wildflower.

We will be in Hot Springs Saturday. We have to hike fifteen miles tomorrow if we are going to be in town on time.

Most of the day, we have been hiking downhill, which I prefer, but my sister doesn't like descents. We crossed Harmon Den Mountain but did not take the detour to the summit. After climbing, a stile we arrived at Max Patch. The elevation on this bald is 4629 feet.

Max Patch is the most wonderful bald. It's an old logging camp and homestead. The summit was used in early years to graze sheep and cattle. The summit was also used to land small planes. With the help of volunteers, mowing, and having controlled burns, we can enjoy its bald appearance and grassy meadows.

The summit, at 4,629 feet, offers panoramic views of the Smoky Mountains to the south and Mt. Mitchell to the east.

All day, we seemed to be crossing streams. It was a pretty hike today, with everything in bloom.

There are only five in the shelter tonight. Everyone else is pushing ahead to Hot Springs. Roaring Fork Shelter is a log shelter built amid a thicket of rhododendrons. We have two resident squirrels. I hope they retire when we do. We slept in the shelter tonight.

We hiked 11.3 miles today.

Friday-On our way down the mountain, three and a half miles short of Hot Springs, LaTripper took a fall. She was so excited to see town in the distance that she started picking up speed. She took a hard fall, hitting her face very hard. She got up bleeding from the nose. I laid her against the bank and began treating her. Her glasses had cut her nose, and it appeared she had broken her nose. Her first comment was "I don't care how I look because I am going to have a cold beer tonight, maybe even two." Frank came along at that time and offered to carry some of LaTripper's pack. He gave her his hanky to help stop the bleeding. Frank stayed with us all the way down to make sure we were safe. When we got to the medical center, it was about to close. They took my sister in anyway. She ended up with five stitches, and they confirmed she had probably broken her nose.

We hiked 14.9 miles today.

The rumor in town was that there were no vacancies anywhere. Trip's dad offered us a bed in his hotel room and said he would camp out on the floor. We all headed for Paddler's Pub for dinner and the drink LaTripper so wanted. We were sitting at the table, with a few other hikers, and to my surprise, I saw Eddie sitting at the bar. He had gotten in a day early and was just hanging out. I was never so happy to see someone in all my life. He is the love of my life. I would not be out here if it were not for the love and support he gives me. Eddie shuttled everyone who would fit in the van all over town to shop, post office, laundry, and anywhere they wanted to go.

On Sunday, Ed took four of us north to Allen Gap to slack-pack, fifteen miles south to Hot Springs. Tomorrow, he will take us back to Allen Gap, and we will hike north from there. It was nice to hike all day without a forty-pound pack on my back. I finally checked my e-mail on Saturday, and I had forty-one emails from friends and family. It was also nice to see all the hikers in town whom we have been hiking with on and off.

Monday-It was very hard to say good-bye to Eddie. He will meet me again a bit farther along.

We had a gradual elevation gain today. We went from 2,235 feet to 4,780 feet. LaTripper is not doing well today. Her energy level is down. I feel better after a day in town, but I'm out of sorts today. I keep losing my focus on why I'm out here. I guess it's normal to have these feelings occasionally. I hope tomorrow is better for me.

We hiked 11.6 miles to the Jerry Cabin Shelter.

Tuesday-We had beautiful views from the Basset Memorial. The memorial honors a 1968 thru-hiker who was one of the first fifty hikers to ever hike the AT. His ashes are buried there.

We had a really good scramble over the boulder field and Big Butt Mountains. There are lots of beautiful grassy knolls in this section of the trail.

We stopped for lunch at Flint Mountain Shelter.

It was a hard hike today. We had continuous climbs again today. We saw some beautiful waterfalls coming out of Devil Fork Gap, North Carolina.

It rained tonight, and I slept like a baby. After hiking 6.8 miles, we set up camp beyond Devil Fork Gap

Indian Pipes

Ghost Flowers
Beneath the pines, a cluster of tiny Indian Pipes grows without chlorophyll, white against the wet soil like small Cherokee children, torn from freedom and the mountains, paled in faded ledges by rocky streams.

Bettie M. Sellers

Wednesday-It's May first, and what a beautiful morning. We had lots of climbs again today. We hiked the two and a half miles to Hog Back Ridge Shelter, cooked breakfast, and relaxed before heading out again. We hung our tents and gear up to dry while we had lunch. Water supplies seem to be getting harder to find.

The 5,516-foot Big Bald, a mountain on the Tennessee and North Carolina border, has one of the best views of any peak on the trail.[3]

Big Bald is the highest mountain on the trail between Roan Mountain and the Smokies.

White flowers, called fringed phacelia or summer snow, are all over this bald. I would like to put my tent up here tonight, but they are

---

[3] A bald is an open grassy area on top of a mountain.

calling for thunderstorms again. The climb up to the top was challenging but well worth it. The bald helped me to remember all the reasons I'm out here, hiking the trail. You could never see sights like this if you were touring by car. We have sixteen more miles to Erwin and another town day.

We hiked 17.9 miles, which is the most we have hiked so far. We made it to Bald Mountain Shelter.[4]

Thursday-We hiked a much easier terrain today. I enjoyed Spivey Gap. We took a lunch break and cooled off in the river. Another hiker told us that someone fell asleep while sitting in the water and had been bitten by a copperhead last year.

We arrived early at the shelter tonight. The water source was two-tenths of a mile south of the shelter, but we missed it. Naturally, it was on a hill, so back down we went. We should make it to Erwin tomorrow for another town day.

I'm seeing a lot of wild columbine, mountain laurels, and rhododendrons in this area. I will miss the wildflowers when I get farther north.

We stopped at No Business Knob Shelter after hiking 10.5 miles.

Friday-It was an easy day today.

When you cross the Nolichucky River on the Chestoa Bridge, you are walking in the paths of our forefathers. Davy Crockett and Andrew Jackson are known to have attended frontier gatherings along the river here.

We are so glad to be in Erwin, Tennessee, and we decided to stay at Uncle Johnny's Nolichucky Hostel for the night.

Our mail drop arrived, with all our goodies. I checked my e-mail and was so surprised to hear from everyone. I hope everyone keeps the e-mails coming. It is a very good motivator. I miss all of you, and I will carry each of you in my heart every step of the way, even if it is in spirit only.

We have hiked more than 300 miles of our hike, and we are still going strong. Most days are good, but a few are very challenging.

---

[4] Max Patch is an example of one of the many balds along the Trail.

Overall, we are still enjoying being out here. We are going to take Saturday off and spend the day exploring Erwin and catching up on some much-needed rest. Uncle Johnny shuttled us to town to go shopping and to get some dinner. We met several hikers for dinner. It's nice to relax over some real food instead of all the camp food. We were going to rent a bike and go riding around town, but they were not in very good repair. I spoke with Ed today. He might be able to meet us at Curly Maple Gap Shelter for lunch.

A lot of hikers go to Miss Janet's house. The talk on the trail is that Miss Janet and Uncle Johnny's have a bit of a feud going. Check the data books to see if Uncle Johnny's is still open.

We hiked 6.3 miles to town.

Sunday-I had a perfect day today. It's amazing how one day of rest can make such a difference. It was so lush and beautiful coming out of Erwin. We hiked along the stream for three hours. There are not as many flowers, but the mountain laurels are starting to bloom, and a few purple rhododendrons are beginning to open. I'm still not seeing much wildlife. I love hiking early in the morning. The birds are singing so sweetly, as if I am the only one in the woods, and they are singing to me alone.

We are a half day behind Amy and Shawn. I hope we can catch up with them. I so enjoyed their company.

We got down to the road, and there was a note for us from Miriam and her daughter. They had prepared a large picnic for the hikers at the top of Beauty Spot Mountain. She thought we had left Erwin Saturday and stayed at Curly Maple Gap Shelter that night. We would only have had a seven-mile hike. By the time we hiked to the top, it was 4:15 p.m. The remaining hikers at the top said we missed them by five minutes. They had parked on the north side of the mountain and walked up from there. That was so very special and thoughtful of them. I'm so sorry we missed the good food and the companionship.

Beauty Spot is a lot like Max Patch. I would like to come back in the future and spend more time up there.

Our highest climb today was 4,437 feet. We have some big climbs tomorrow. We will be climbing up to 5,180 feet. Hopefully, I will have the same energy I had today.

I'm only wearing one knee brace now. My left knee seems to be fine. I take the right one off on the level terrain, which isn't very often.

It's nice to be away from the shelters for the night. Jason and his dog are camping nearby.

We set up camp at Deep Gap. We hiked 12.1 miles today.

Monday-I had a good night's sleep last night. It cooled off nicely, and it was peacefully quiet.

I left camp by 8:00 a.m. We hiked out of the gap from 4,120 feet up to 5,180 feet right from camp.

The weather was nice and cool today. Unaba Mountain is quite remarkable. I hiked alone for two hours through the magnificent red spruce. They say red spruce is rare south of New England. I think the forest is a place to get lost in and enjoy the peace and serenity of it. I was so at peace with myself being in this beautiful, serene spot. It was like a magical place. The forest floor was like walking on carpet. Except for the white AT blazes, you could not tell where the trail was. It almost appeared undisturbed. A strange thing though, I did not hear any birds while I was in the forest. Once I started my descent, they started singing to me again.

I have heard that shrews are found in this area. I did not see any, but I'm told that they are the smallest mammals found. Some weigh as little as a dime. They look like mice with pointed noses, smaller eyes, and almost nonexistent ears, but they are not rodents. Their bite is venomous, similar to a cobra. I learn something new every day.

It was a long day with lots of ascents and descents. We finally caught up with Grayson, Amy, and Shawn. It is always so much fun to have them along for the hike. They are going to hike up Roan Mountain with us tomorrow. Roan Mountain, Tennessee is at 6,285 feet.

The trail does not go all the way up to the summit. This should be the last time the AT climbs above 6,000 feet until we reach Mount Washington in New Hampshire.

We were just starting down after a good climb when we ran into Sir James. He was going the opposite direction and stopped us. He was carrying two cases of cold beer in his backpack and offering a cold one to everyone he passed. Of course, we accepted. They weren't that cold, but they tasted like a little bit of heaven. My sister drank hers so fast; she had a bit of a buzz. She continued down the mountain singing at the top of her lungs.

I just can't say enough about the outstanding beauty of all the varieties of flowers. We came over the summit to find the whole valley full with brilliant yellow star grass flowers. The star grass has six petals in a star shape at the top of a long spike stem. If that wasn't enough, all the trees were in bloom as well. They appeared to be apple trees, but I'm not sure what they were.

We ended up at Clyde Smith Shelter in North Carolina. We completed thirteen miles today.

Tuesday-We have completed 375 miles so far. Every time I look at my total miles, I'm amazed that I'm still going along this long, long trail. I never dreamed I would make it this far and still want to keep going. I still love being out here on the trail even more than ever.

We broke camp early for our ascent to Roan Mountain. We started at an altitude of 4,400 feet and climbed up to 6,285 feet to the summit. As the AT ascends, there is an interesting progression from a typical southern hardwood forest at Hughes Gap to a balsam-fir-spruce forest reminiscent of the AT in Maine and New Hampshire.

The Catawba rhododendron garden, atop the 6,327-foot peak of the massive Roan Mountain, covers an area of six hundred acres. They comprise the largest display of blooming rhododendrons to be found anywhere in the world today. No camera can capture the glorious and magnificent beauty of the giant Rhododendron catawbiense when in their peak of bloom.

Over Mountain Shelter

Over Mountain Shelter is a large red barn that has been converted for hikers and can be seen long before arriving. These awesome balds offer some of the most breathtaking views. There are two floors for hikers to set up on. We chose the top floor so we would have a better view. That was probably a mistake since the mice seem to gravitate to the top floor. The barn was once used as the backdrop for the movie Winter People, and the movie stars in this movie were Kurt Russell, Kelly McGillis, and Lloyd Bridges.

We had lunch at Carver Gap. Going north from the gap, we climbed over Jane Bald and Grassy Ridge. We took the side trail to the summit of Grassy Ridge, and the views were spectacular.

The rocks through this area are the oldest to be seen on the entire AT, estimated to be 2.5 billion years old.

We hiked 12.4 miles today and enjoyed a wonderful night in the Over Mountain Shelter.

The Roan Mountain Rhododendron Festival is held every June. You can enjoy demonstrations and entertainment all day. They have a variety of arts, crafts, food, and drink. It is well worth the stop or something to come back for in the future. The Roan Mountain Citizens Club sponsors the event with proceeds going toward scholarships and other community projects and events. There is a scenic drive through this area. Check the data books for directions.

Roan Mountain is a tiny friendly village nestled beneath the magnificent heights of the mountain that gave it its name. The climate is wonderful, and the people are delightful and friendly!

Roan Mountain is arguably the coldest spot, year-round, on the southern section of the Trail. At the top is a clearing where the former Cloudland Hotel stood. The North Carolina and Tennessee border ran through the center of their ballroom. It was demolished in 1915 after loggers harvested all the fir and spruce on the mountain. There is a road up the other side of the mountain.

Wednesday-After leaving the shelter, we hiked over several balds and walked along the ridge for several miles. I really enjoyed Little Hump and Hump Mountain. Hump Mountain, at 5,587 feet, is a spectacular vista, with expansive views in all directions. The unique profile of Hump Mountain is visible in clear weather from many parts of northeast Tennessee. From US 19E to the summit is an elevation gain of 2,880 feet.

It was mostly downhill from there. We were in camp early tonight. We spent some time washing up in the stream. That was a nice treat.

We pitched our tents near the water tonight. Hopefully, the gurgling water will lull me to sleep. I did not sleep well last night because of all the snoring and the mice scurrying all around me. I will be glad to be in my tent tonight. We have a long day tomorrow, so we will retire early.

We hiked 8.2 miles to Apple House Shelter. The shelter was first constructed in 1952 to store explosives for a quarry in the hollow. The Tennessee Eastman Hiking Club and the Forest Service later rebuilt it.

Thursday-It was a very long day with a lot of climbs. In the morning, we meandered through the farmland with the cows, horses, and donkeys. We were dodging cow patties for quite a while. It's a shame the wild roses are not in bloom yet. The whole valley is full of wild rose bushes. LaTripper counted twelve climbs, which resulted in a scramble downhill each time, of course. We seemed to be crossing over streams every time we reached the valley. Most of the descents were very muddy and slippery. We were lucky to make it to camp without any falls. There is a rumor that the trail will be rerouted next year to avoid some of the climbs and stream crossings.

There were several places where we could have stopped, with so many roads crossing in this area, but we decided to keep on hiking. We will be in town tomorrow and have enough supplies until then. At US 19E, we could have had a good lunch at the King of the Road Restaurant and Steak House. It was a half-mile walk to the restaurant. A two-and-a-half-mile walk would have taken us into Elk Park, North Carolina, where there are several restaurants and grocery services. We could have stopped at Mountain Harbor Bed and Breakfast which was only three-tenths of a mile off the trail, but since tomorrow was a town day, we pushed on.

We got to camp around 7:00 p.m. It was getting dark by then so by the time we did all our chores and ate, it was time for bed.

We stopped at Moreland Gap Shelter in Tennessee and hiked 14.3 miles today.

Friday-We only hiked 5.8 miles today.

On the way down White Rocks Mountain, we came to a blue-blazed trail to the Coon Den Falls. We were so anxious to get into town that we bypassed this photo opportunity.

We hiked with Grayson, Juicy Shoes, and Shamrock today. We walked two-tenths of a mile up Dennis Cove Road to the Kincora Hiking Hostel. The hostel is a log cabin and offers bunk beds, tree house, tenting on the lawn, kitchen facilities, and laundry facilities. They offer free shuttles to town daily. The hostel is owned and operated by Bob and Pat Peoples.

When I got to the hostel, I called Ed. I was surprised to find him only half an hour from there. I walked down to the road to watch for him and was never so excited to see the old white van come rolling over the hill. Ed parked at the hostel, and joined everyone inside. After getting settled, we all piled into Ed's van and headed for Hampton, Tennessee. Hampton has just about anything a hiker would need. There is an Internet café if you need to catch up with friends and family.

We all went for lunch and pigged out on some good town food. I caught my sister smiling at me while she was chatting with the other hikers at her table. I asked her what she was smiling at, and she said how cute it was to see Ed and me just chattering away. She said I did not stop talking for the last half —an hour. I was so excited to share all my adventures with Ed I just felt like I was going to run out of time to tell him all my adventures. After lunch, everyone piled back into the van, and Ed ran us all over town to shop for groceries and anywhere anyone needed to go.

Saturday-LaTripper and I took the day off from hiking the trail. I decided to spend the day with Ed and organize and clean my pack while Lorelei decided to do trail maintenance. Pat Peoples and the AT club members were looking for volunteers to do some trail maintenance on a section close to the hostel. Lorelei and most of the other hikers worked all day and were exhausted when they returned. They all received a patch to display on their pack and the satisfaction of having given something back to the AT.

While we were in town, we shopped for dinner supplies, and tonight, we had spaghetti with a huge salad and fresh vegetables.

Sunday-Ed drove us south to where the trail intersects US 321. We slack-packed north to Laurel Fork Shelter and decided to take a lunch break before continuing on. It felt so good to just have a lightweight day pack on. We need to slack-pack more often.

We hiked a short blue-blazed trail into the Laurel Fork Gorge and then we hiked up to Laurel Falls, a fifty-foot waterfall. The wild and rugged Laurel Fork Gorge is located in the Pond Mountain Wilderness in Carter County, Tennessee.

We enjoyed playing on the rocks and cooling off while Shawn, Amy, and some of the others decided to go swimming. The rhododendrons and orange azaleas were in full bloom. This was such a breathtaking spot to just sit and contemplate life.

We only hiked nine glorious miles today, and we stayed another night at the Kincora Hostel.

Monday-Ed took LaTripper, Shawn, Amy, and me to breakfast before we left. It was really hard to say good-bye to Eddie again today. He said he would try to meet me in Damascus.

Ed drove us to US 321, where we hiked north yesterday. We started out with a light rain and hiked most of the day with beautiful views of Watauga Lake. We filled our water bottles at Shook Branch Recreation Area. We enjoyed a short break at the picnic tables. It's a nice area for a day picnic. They have restrooms and a beach for swimming.

We passed by the Watauga Lake Shelter and continued north about one mile to the Watauga Dam. The AT crosses the top of the dam, which is on the Watauga River.

The dam was completed in 1948 and displaced about seven hundred people living along the riverbanks. The Watauga Dam was one of the first earth-filled hydroelectric dams built in the US.

We made it to Vandeventer Shelter before the deluge started. The shelter was full at three in the afternoon, so we sat the storm out and decided to continue on for a few more miles. We were in such a hurry to set up camp before the bad weather came in we missed quite a few good views. We were able to set up camp before we had any more rain. Tonight is supposed to be the first cold night in a while. They are calling for more rain, and it's already getting foggy. I had sent my sleeping bag liner, gloves, fleece pants, and a few other things home. I hope it isn't too cold tonight.

We hiked four miles north of the Vandeventer Shelter and decided to camp in the woods. We hiked a total of 12.4 miles today.

Tuesday-I woke up from the best night's sleep I have had in a long time. It was in the forties last night; with the wind —chill, it was probably closer to thirty degrees. I was warm enough though.

Today was an absolutely perfect day for hiking. It stayed in the forties and was windy all morning. I love this type of weather for hiking. My sister prefers it to be much warmer.

We stopped at the Grindstaff Monument for a break.

The story is told that Nick Grindstaff was robbed of all his money while traveling west. He returned to Iron Mountain, where he lived for forty-six years, becoming a famous hermit. Visiting relatives accidentally killed his pet rattlesnake. This is said to have been his only friend. A plaque was placed in his honor by relatives.

We continued on to Double Springs Gap Shelter for lunch and then on to Low Gap, which is located at US 421, near Shady Valley, Tennessee. Others stopped for the night, and we sat around a campfire and enjoyed the evening. I enjoyed the solitude my tents give me. It is a welcome change from shelter life. We hiked 14.5 miles today.

Clingman's Dome, Tennessee

VIRGINIA: SOUTHWEST

May 15-June 1, 2002

Virginia is the longest state with 544 miles of trail. The state flower is the American dogwood, and the state bird is the northern cardinal.

Wednesday-We decided to continue on and passed the Abingdon Gap Shelter. We hiked with Amy and Shawn all day. Three miles before reaching Damascus, we crossed the border into Virginia. It was an easy hike from there into Damascus.

We hiked 14.8 miles to make it into town.

We all set up our tents down by the river. This was the last year the town allowed the hikers to camp by the river. Since 2002, the hikers had to walk out of town, and there was an area behind the school cleared for them. This area is no longer available either. In 2010, they cleared this spot for ball fields. If you plan on staying at a bed and breakfast, you need to make reservations ahead of time. The Place Hostel, provided by the Damascus First United Methodist Church, has a two-day limit.

There are numerous restaurants in town. The data book lists phone numbers and other information that will assist you in making reservations ahead of time. Damascus is a good town to replenish your supplies or send home anything you don't need until the weather turns cold again.

I found Eddie waiting for me in town. I left my tent up but will sleep in the van with Eddie, of course. It is so nice to have him run us around town again. We are thinking about staying through the weekend.

The parade at Trail Days was extra special this year since it was in honor of the passing of Earl Shaffer, the first AT thru-hiker. Other events throughout the year include the Fourth of July celebrations, which they call the Beaver Jam. I would love to come back to this festivity.

As you walk through town on US 58, you are actually walking along the AT. If you were up to an extra three-and-a-half-mile walk, you could check out the Backbone Rock formation that VA 716 tunnels through.

We took three days off this time. This is the longest layover since I started hiking. I hope I can get motivated to start hiking again.

Hiker's Parade at Trail Days

Sunday-I really enjoyed Damascus and the time with Ed and friends. I met quite a few hikers we had seen throughout our hike. Most of the music was bluegrass, which is so appropriate for the south. I did some dancing with Ed. I tried to dance a two-step, but I was not very good.

The Virginia Creeper Trail runs along the old railroad for about thirty-three. It began as a Native American footpath and was later used by the pioneers. The AT shares the Creeper Trail as you go north out of Damascus for a short distance and picks it up again for about ten miles farther up the trail.

It was an easy walk out of town. It was so hard to say good bye to Ed. This will be my last visit with him for the rest of the summer. He is heading for California with his friend Ron. My knee is bothering me today. I think I'll do better if I hike every day and keep it from swelling up. It was in the sixties most of the day. We had a cold front come in on Saturday and it dropped into the thirties overnight. My sister is not doing well physically and mentally. She is very homesick again. She does not do well when it turns cold.

We hiked 11.7 miles and set up camp by the pond tonight.

Monday-We had ice on our water this morning, and I had condensation inside my tent from the cold air outside and the heat inside. LaTripper was cold all night and in bad spirits today. We left camp at 10:00 a.m. It never got above forty degrees all day. I love to hike in the colder temperatures, but LaTripper was not happy. I feel like I have more energy. I seemed to fly up White Mountain, which was a 2,420-foot gain. White Mountain's elevation is about 5,500 feet. This is one of Virginia's highest mountains. If you are coming through this area at the end of the month, you can participate in the ramp festival. They have a ramp-eating contest. Some of the hikers use ramps to season their camp food. It's similar to onions or wild leeks in taste, but not in looks. I have not tried it yet.

As you reach the top, you suddenly walk out to a breathtaking open meadow with views that seem to go on forever. Everything is so lush and green now. The flowers on the bald are simply stupendous. There were lots of bluetts, violets, and an abundant amount of fringed phacelia, better known as summer snow. It was snowing on the climb up the mountain and all the way down the other side. I think we are in for a long, cold night.

It was so cold tonight that I was in my tent by 8:00 p.m., and it's still snowing outside. It is suggested that you do not send your winter clothes home until you finish climbing Mount Rogers. Well, I took a chance and sent my gloves and fleece pants home. I hiked all day with socks on my hands to try and keep them warm. LaTripper had sent all of her long pants home as well. I wore all my rain gear to bed to try and stay warm. I expected to see quite a few campers since everyone was leaving from Damascus, but we only had three campers tonight.

We stopped for the night at Elk Garden Campsites. I have been told that elk grazed this area along with bison and mountain lions, many, many years ago. You may be lucky to see a black bear, wild turkey, or even a deer or two as you approach VA 600.

We completed 12.1 miles today.

Tuesday-I learned a valuable lesson last night. I usually hang my water filter out at night to air it out. When I got up this morning, the filter had frozen, and I was unable to filter water for the day. I was up before my sister this morning and went to check out the weather. I took a walk to the parking lot. I saw the most beautiful yellow and black finches filling the branches of an old maple tree in the parking lot. I'm surprised to see so many of them for such a cold morning.

I guess numerous day hikers use this area. In the parking lot was a sign that read: "Pack it in, pack it out," and underneath it were three bags of garbage. It's a shame to see how careless and thoughtless people can be.

While sitting here and enjoying the morning as I'm waiting for my sister to wake up, I'm racking my brain to come up with a way to put words to my experience. I saw a sign that helps me put it all into perspective. "To be completely self-sufficient with everything I need on my back."

This describes it so well. Also, the ability to experience solitude you just don't find out in the real world. The trail is a place to escape the pressures of everyday life, to be a part of this untamed nature, and to have a chance to experience the natural beauty and sheer power of nature.

I've been up since seven thirty, and it's not warming up much. There is a sheet of ice on the cars in the parking lot. The sun is up, the birds are singing, and the cows are calling me. It's neat how you can come out of the wilderness and walk across pastureland with cows, and the next thing you know, you're back in the dense and remote forest again.

My sister is not feeling well today. She said she couldn't deal with the cold for another day. I think she is very homesick. After about forty-five minutes, we finally got a ride back to Damascus. There were two men coming from the opposite direction, and they stopped to see if we were okay. I told them my sister wasn't feeling well, and we needed to get back into town. They said if they were going our way, they would give us a ride and headed on. A few moments later, they were back. They said they felt bad leaving us in the cold and offered to take us to town. We offered to pay them for gas, but they refused.

We stayed at the Lazy Fox Bed and Breakfast right on the river. Since Trail Days were over, we were the only ones at the Lazy Fox. I would recommend this facility to anyone. It is worth every penny. I soaked in the tub for so long I was all shriveled up when I got out. Such luxury! Sis took a long nap and woke up feeling better so we decided to go out for a while and explore town. I can't wait for breakfast tomorrow morning.

Wednesday-Breakfast was more than I ever expected. The owners put so much work into preparing such a treat for just the two of us. Everything was homemade, from the apple butter to the muffins. I ate so much it's a wonder I was able to go back out and hike.

We found someone to shuttle us back to the trail, where we dropped off yesterday. We did not get started until one thirty in the afternoon. We planned on stopping at Thomas Knob Shelter since we had heard the sunsets from there were breathtaking.

I enjoyed the hike up Mount Rogers. We had an elevation gain from 965 feet to 5,400 feet. You can take the Susan Spillane Side Trail if you want to go to the summit, which is at 5,729 feet. If you are lucky, you will see a Weller salamander. They are a dark blue-black with gold splotches on their backs. They are endangered in this area and can usually only be found above 5,000 feet.

Our friend Brian and his dog are leaving the trail from here. He is having some problems with his feet. I will miss them both. I hope he gets back on when his feet have healed.

We had such beautiful views from up here. We sat out on the rocks until it got too cold to sit out any longer. Thomas Knob is a nice shelter with an enclosed loft. We decided to stay up top. There were only four of us in the shelter tonight. It was a nice change and warmer today. This should be our last cold night, hopefully. It was warmer hiking today than yesterday. It was sunny, and there was no snow today.

We only hiked 4.2 miles today.

Thursday-If I had to rate my hike today on a scale of one to ten, it would be a ten. I know I've said this before, however, today had to be some of the most beautiful scenery I have experienced since I began my hike. I would love to come back to this area for the fall festival.

We had the bluest skies today with lots of sunshine. I have never seen the terrain change so quickly in just a few miles. One minute I'm hiking through pastureland with horses roaming wild and grazing within an arm's reach, and the next thing I know, I'm in the woods again. Fifteen minutes later, I'm back in the open pastureland. I loved the rocky cliffs. That was the highlight of my day. We stopped at the Wise Shelter for our lunch. There was a tunnel at one of the rocks that we climbed called Fat Man Squeeze Tunnel. I cheated and went around instead of trying to squeeze through. I loved the hike along Wilburn Ridge. The wide-open views were spectacular.

Grayson Highlands State Park is similar to the grasslands of Montana. The park is located adjacent to Mount Rogers National Recreation Area and is a part of the Jefferson National Forest. The park was established in 1965 and contains a total of 4,822 acres. The state park is musically notable as the home for the Grayson Highlands Fall Festival as well as weekly jam sessions by local folk musicians.

The balds are inhabited by a herd of introduced ponies allowed to run wild within the confines of the park and have lived on the balds of Wilburn Ridge in Grayson Highlands for over fifty years. The ponies are very accustomed to humans and rarely halt their grazing as you pass close by. One of them kept trying to get my watch off my arm. I think he could smell the Snickers bar in my pocket and kept nudging me.

Each year, park officials round up the herd and check for health problems.

There are quite a few hikers setting up their tents tonight. We hiked eleven miles to Old Orchard Shelter.

Friday-Well, it was another great day.

I saw a deer about half a mile from the shelter. He just stood there and checked us out but did not run away.

We hiked until 8:15 p.m. tonight, which is late for us. We hitched a ride into Troutdale to shop for three days' worth of food to hold us until we reach our next town and mail drop. It's always nice to get a shower and leave with clean clothes. I'm feeling much more comfortable about hitchhiking. I seem to be setting up my tent more often now. I really enjoy the solitude of being in my little tent, tucked away under a tree somewhere, or, if I'm lucky, along a nice bubbling stream. We're still behind Grayson, Amy, and Shawn. I hope we catch up with them soon.

I love Virginia. Everything is so lush and green now, and the mountain laurel is in full bloom. Mountain laurel flowers vary from pure white to pink, with some red markings throughout. When in full bloom, they can fill an entire mountainside with such a beautiful display.

I have hiked more than five hundred miles to date.

We stopped at the Trimpi Shelter after hiking for 14.2 miles.

Saturday-I called Eddie and was sad to hear that he was leaving with his friend for California until the end of summer.

I have my tent set up again tonight under the pines, with the frogs lulling me to sleep. I decided to leave my tent flap open so I could watch the full moon. They are calling for thunderstorms tonight. Hope to get up early for a long hike tomorrow.

I heard coyotes last night in the distance for about twenty minutes. I wasn't concerned, but it is a very eerie sound when you're alone in the dark.

We hiked 10.5 miles to the Partnership Shelter. This shelter is the shelter of shelters. You could call it the Ritz Carlton of shelters. This is the first shelter I have seen with showers. We don't often find a treat like this. It is close to a visitor center so they probably see numerous weekend hikers. We called for pizza to be delivered and split it four-ways. Four dollars for pizza and a cold soda was quite a treat from our boring trail food.

Sunday-The forest floor is gently swaying with ferns, and the rhododendrons are alive with bloom. There is a nice cool breeze today. It's been a nice gentle hike, and I'm enjoying the early morning solitude. It's so beautiful walking through tunnels of rhododendrons and flame azaleas, which are now in full bloom.

I saw two grouse today. The first one was chattering away at me while protecting her young chicks. A few minutes later, I was startled as one took off from the bushes with such haste that it made a terrible racket. Next thing I know, there was a rabbit scurrying back and forth across the trail. I expect she was protecting her young babies somewhere in the bushes. I feel like I'm in a zoo out here today.

I thought about my mom a lot today. She loved this country and would have enjoyed seeing all the blooming trees and flowers today. I hope she is looking down on me and can see how happy and serene I am to be out here.

We stopped at the Chatfield Shelter for lunch. This shelter is named after Louise Meroney Chatfield, a conservationist and Piedmont Appalachian Trail Hikers Club founder.

Shortly north of the shelter, along VA 615, we stopped at the Settlers Museum. The farmstead and visitor's center include exhibits of rural life at the time the valley was settled. We walked through a schoolhouse that was built in 1880. It was fun exploring the schoolhouse and pretending we were in the good old days. The original school books were still in place.

At the crossing of Interstate 81, we walked a short distance to the Barn Restaurant. The restaurant is right on the trail with a Texaco gas station nearby for a few supplies if you are running short until your next mail drop. Atkins, Virginia, is a short 3.2-mile hitch if you are in need of supplies.

We have climbed over at least seven stiles today.

Try working your way over one of these with a thirty-pound pack on your back. The stiles take you over fences as you cross through pastureland. It gets easier after the first few, and you establish your own technique.

The Appalachian Trail as well as Virginia's Wildlife and Birding Trail runs through The Settlers Museum of Southwest Virginia. It's a good opportunity to learn about life in the mountains over one hundred years ago. Take time to visit this sixty-seven-acre open-air museum and learn the story of the people who settled the area. You can view a restored nineteenth-century living history farm complete with farmhouse and eight original outbuildings. The AT passes very close to the restored 1894 one-room Linda Mood schoolhouse. We spent time in the school house and felt the pull to be part of the past. The old school books are still in place at each desk.

You have to get water nine-tenths of a mile south of shelter. There is no water at the shelter. The next water source is three and a half miles north.

I'm sleeping in the shelter tonight since they are calling for rain. This shelter has limited tent sites. We stopped at the Davis Path Shelter for the night after a 14.3-mile hike.

Monday-We had lots of climbing today, but I'm doing so much better than I did when I first started my hike. We got caught in a heavy downpour today and decided not to put our rain gear on. I was already hot, and the rain felt good. We stopped at Knot Maul Branch Shelter for a break and to dry out. This shelter is named for the knotty wood settlers used for mauls for their farm work. I ended up taking a two-hour nap. From there, we continued on for about three more miles.

Our water source is usually a running stream. Most of the springs are dried up. I miss the good spring water we were finding in the early days.

I followed a huge cow down the path today. She was just meandering along at her own speed, which was super slow. I clapped my poles together to get her moving after I made sure it was not a bull, of course. She finally wandered off, and we could continue down the trail, carefully stepping around the cow patties.

I slipped on the trail today and caught myself by grabbing onto a small tree. I had a death grip on that tree to keep from sliding down the side of the mountain. There I was, hanging off the side, hugging a tree with thirty-five pounds on my back and ready to drop over the edge. I started laughing so hard I couldn't move and was about to wet my pants. As usual, LaTripper came to the rescue and helped pull me around and back onto the trail. I was fine except for a few abrasions from hanging on so tightly to the tree.

Today was a repeat of yesterday. We meandered for miles through farmlands, then back into the woods for a short distance, then back through the meadows again. It seems like we are always crossing roads or streams since we got into Virginia. We crossed the north fork of the Holston River today. There was a high watermark where the river can rise five feet over the bridge at times. Thank goodness it was not flooded today. We would have had to turn around and find a detour around the area, adding several miles to our day.

We got into camp late because we took a two-hour nap today. We set up camp in the woods just after the Lick Creek. I enjoy getting into camp and sitting around with the other hikers. When you get into camp for the night, someone you hiked with several days ago may be there for the night. It's so much fun to catch up with their daily hike. We still have not caught up with Shawn and Amy. I think they may be too far ahead now.

We are camping in the woods near Lick Creek. We hiked 14.6 miles today. We have completed one-quarter of the trail now. I am so ecstatic.

Tuesday-We had another day with a lot of climbs. Water sources are getting harder to find. We are in the middle of a drought, and I am concerned about finding water as we get further into the summer. We were lucky to find a muddy stream, which filled up my filter quite quickly. Someone shared a tip with me that will help prolong the life of your filters. Put a coffee filter around the sediment filter to catch most of the sediment. You will catch quite a bit of dirt. I think I will change filters when I have the chance. Sis and I are sharing one filter, and it takes forever to pump the water through when it starts to clog up.

The terrain is similar to the last two days. The hike to Chestnut Knob Shelter took us through green meadows and up onto the ridges. The shelter was a former fire warden's cabin and was once called "the cave" but now has Plexiglas windows to let in some light. It was renovated in 1994. The elevation at the shelter is 4,410 feet and overlooks an unusual geologic feature, which was the Vanderbilt's' first choice for their Biltmore estate, later constructed near Asheville, North Carolina. It is a large crater-shaped depression surrounded on all sides by a high ridge that the AT follows for about eight miles.

Water is scarce in this area. You can get water just before you get to the shelter or you can go east about fifty yards on an old Jeep road. We found water here, but it was limited. If you can't locate water here, there is usually water at Walker's Gap, which is a little over one mile north. We stopped for lunch and a nap and started back out around 4:00 p.m., hiking for another three hours.

Southern Living Magazine had reporters doing interviews and photos at Walkers Gap. They did a short interview with me, but I don't think I will make the magazine.

We followed the ridge for two hours after hiking out of Walkers Gap. We decided to camp on top of the ridge and found a nice spot tucked away in the trees. We have a nice breeze tonight. It should be good sleeping here. We hiked 9.5 miles today.

Wednesday—I think I might get a radio to break up the hours of just walking all day long, but I think I would miss the sounds of nature all around me. The songbirds are always singing so sweetly.

My mind goes constantly as I hike along. I think for the first time in my life I am learning who I really am. I think about my strengths and weaknesses, my children, grandchildren, and Eddie all the time. Your mind never seems to shut down.

Coming down off the ridge today, I saw bear droppings and signs they had been grubbing for food. I haven't seen one yet, but I am starting to see a lot of snakes. I found some lilies of the valley today. They smell heavenly as you walk through them. I didn't realize they grew wild.

We walked along Little Wolf Creek for several miles today. I think we crossed it ten times, if not more. They do have a high water trail if the water is too high for crossing. It wouldn't take much rain to flood this creek. Food supply is getting low, but we will replenish them tomorrow. We got into camp early tonight. We decided to set up camp in the woods near Little Wolf Creek.

We only hiked 9.5 miles today.

Thursday-We had an easy day today. We went into Bland, Virginia by way of US 52 to pick up supplies. As we approached the parking lot, we were excited to see a true trail Angel waiting for all the hikers. I had a cold soda, two Little Debbie cakes, and an orange. As if that wasn't enough, they offered us a ride to town. We were planning on hitching a ride the three miles to town. When we got to town, they drove us all over town so we could take care of our errands. You can't even imagine how good Dairy Queen ice cream tastes after weeks of trail food.

My sister and I were corresponding with a couple, prior to beginning our hike, through a web site called Trail Journals. Their trail names were Who Cook and her husband was Chef. Later we met them along the trail as they were attempting their thru-hike. The trail angels we met in Bland were their children.

From Bland, it was a long climb up to the shelter. After hiking 8.6 miles, we arrived at the Helveys Mill Shelter. This shelter was relocated to this spot when the AT was moved off Walker Mountain in the 1980s.

Friday-The terrain was gentler today. I think I am ready for a zero day in town. I don't have any stamina today. It's been nine days since we've had a shower and done our laundry. We have to make it to Pearisburg, Virginia for supplies; however, there are numerous roads, with an easy hike to town, if we need to go to town sooner.

LaTripper has a bad blister on her heel and may need to stop sooner.

It's calling for rain tonight. It might cool it off a little bit. We stopped at Jenny Knob Shelter after hiking 9.8 miles today. Jenny Knob Shelter was also relocated when the trail was moved off Walker Mountain.

Saturday-We yellow-blazed about thirty miles to Pearisburg, Virginia, which means we will have to make up the miles in the future.

LaTripper's blister has gotten worse, and she could not hike anymore. We both had run out of medical supplies for her foot. The heat was almost unbearable for both of us. We were ready for a break from the trail. I don't think I will stay out that many days before taking a break again.

We got a hotel this time, and I bet I took a shower for at least half an hour. We ran all our errands and picked up our mail drops and a few additional supplies before heading back to the hotel for some much-needed rest. We had a great dinner of spaghetti and indulged in a couple of cold beers.

While hiking along the last couple of days, I came up with this little ditty. It's amazing how your mind wanders while walking hour after hour.

My Journey

*I'm just a lonely hiker, my name is Trapper Lee
I hike the hills and valleys, my soul forever free.
I'm only one of many, on that northern hike to Maine,
I'm hiking many miles each day, ignoring all the pain.
It's Springer to Katahdin, that's Georgia to Maine,
With my sister and my backpack, and occasionally with pain
It seems we're always climbing that long and rocky Trail,
To the summits and the grasslands, their beauty we must hail.
Now the downward Trail is starting, to the gaps so far below
And the waterfalls go tumbling where the rivers gently flow.
The singing of the birds and rising of the sun
Is the only clock I need out here, my day has just begun.
It's coffee, grits, or oatmeal to fuel our long, hard day,
Snickers, Gorp, and raisins, more fuel throughout the day.
Not every day is perfect; some are really bad.
The aching knees, blistered feet, and bugs that drive you mad.
Now as the day is ending, the good outweighs the bad,
New friendships I am making at each shelter that I stay.
So when I climb Katahdin, this journey will be done
But at each day's beginning, a new one has begun.
Mom, I know you're watching, from the heavens up above
So this journey that I'm taking is for you with all my love.*

Paralee Dawson Hayward

CENTRAL VIRGINIA

June 2-June 23, 2002

Sunday-We took the day off to reorganize our gear and get some much-needed rest. It's always fun to visit with all the other hikers in town.

Monday-We left Pearisburg, Virginia after two days of rest. We had an easy hike today except for the heat and humidity. I just don't have any energy when it's that hot. The bugs are really bad again. They don't bother you until you stop. I finally gave in and bought a radio. I love listening to music when the terrain is boring and just one foot in front of the other.

We crossed over the New River, which is reputed to be the second oldest river in the world after the Nile.

I saw a deer and a raccoon while hiking along the trail. The raccoon was acting strange, and I was concerned about him having rabies. He was just lying in the middle of the path and would not move. We spoke with several other hikers, and they thought the raccoon might be sick.

Our friend Frank saw a bear last night on his way into camp. We found good sources of water today. We had to walk half a mile down to Rice Field Shelter for water.

We decided to camp at Symms Gap Meadow. This mountain meadow has a few sites for tenting with views into West Virginia. A small pond is located downhill from the trail on the West Virginia side of the ridge. It's a beautiful view from our camp of the town down below and the meandering mountain ranges. There were a lot of berry bushes, but the berries were not ripe yet. There are four other campers with us tonight. I hope we have a good sunrise in the morning.

We completed 12.2 miles today.

Tuesday-It's not even summer yet, and it is so hot. We still found water even though there's a drought. I'm drinking more water with the heat, which means I have to carry more, thus additional weight.

We stopped at Pine Swamp Branch Shelter for lunch and a nap. Another hiker told us to watch for rattlesnakes. He saw one in the trail earlier today. The undergrowth is so thick you can barely see the trail. This is perfect snake territory. I came across a turtle in the trail and moved him out of the way. The only other wildlife was a rabbit. I still have not seen any bears.

The shelter is full tonight so I decided to set up my tent even though they were calling for thunderstorms. I am missing Ed's visits, but he should be in Idaho now and then going to California for a few weeks.

Our water source is south of the shelter about two-tenths of a mile and then east on the blue-blaze trail. I didn't realize this and had to go back for water.

We stopped at Bailey Gap Shelter after 11.3 miles.

Wednesday-It's much cooler this morning. I started out early ahead of LaTripper. I've been walking about two hours alone. I just love the early morning hours. LaTripper is not a morning person, and it's been a sensitive subject since the beginning of our hike. After a good night's sleep and a cup of coffee, I'm ready to go.

The chipmunks were very busy this morning. They were scurrying back and forth on the trail. It used to startle me when I would hear them rustling in the bushes. The birds were really active this time of morning, and I think they were singing to me only. When you walk all day, step after step, any disruptions break the monotony. Sis caught up with me, and we enjoyed the day hiking together.

We stopped for a break, and I sat on a log, watching all the birds in the water taking a bath. The puddle we had to filter water from was also the birds' bathtub. The chipmunks were so playful and fun to watch. They enjoyed any crumbs we dropped. The bugs were having lunch on my arms and legs. They were so annoying.

We have several road crossings in this section. After our climb up Wind Rock, elevation 4,100 feet, we continued to hike along the ridge line for most of the day. The terrain is beginning to change again. We are seeing more pines now. I absolutely love this terrain. At the bottom of Lone Pine Peak, the mountain laurel is in full bloom for as far as you can see. We haven't seen many blooming trees or flowers in the last few days.

We stopped at War Spur Shelter for lunch. There was a nice stream running just north of the shelter, and we spent time soaking our hot, tired feet in the cold water. We're camping in a valley near a stream tonight. My first job when I get into camp is to find a tree to hang my food. Then if I'm lucky enough to find a stone, I tie my rope around the rock and throw it over the branch and pray the branch holds, or I don't miss and the rock hits me in the head. I had a rotten branch come down on my head the other day.

We waded in the water and washed up from the sweaty heat of the day. We don't get to do that very often. Our dinners are getting boring. I need to come up with some new ideas. We have a big climb tomorrow so I think it will be an early night. We are the only ones here tonight.

We only hiked 9.1 miles since the heat was wearing us down.

Thursday-There were two deer on the way out of camp today. It was a mother and her fawn. They just stood there and watched me as I did the same. I left ahead of my sister again, and when she caught up with me, she said she had seen her first bear.

It was a hard hike up Rocky Gap, White Rock, and Kelly Knob. We climbed up to an elevation of 3,800 feet by the time we summated White Rock.

It started to rain, and I could hear thunder so we decided to get off the ridge and head for the shelter.

I saw the famous Keffer Oak tree, located at the edge of a pasture. The Keffer Oak is a large white oak measuring over eighteen feet in diameter. The tree is estimated to be about three hundred years old. The Dover Oak along the AT in New York is slightly larger.

It was a good hike downhill to the shelter, but I'm glad we stopped when we did since the storm broke not long after we got to the shelter. The Sarver Hollow Shelter, which is where we stopped for the night, had just been built. The shelter is on the spot where the Sarver cabin remains are still standing. This cabin dates to the 1800s. The water source is a spring located on a steep blue-blazed trail. At the bottom are the remains of the old foundation. If not for the storm, I would love to have explored this area. It has cooled off nicely, and I should have a good night's rest for a change.

Jane and her dog are the only other campers tonight.

We stopped after 11.9 miles.

Friday-I had a wonderful night's sleep. It was a good idea to stop when we did since the trail north was quite rocky and slippery with the rain.

It was an enjoyable walk across the ridge of Sinking Creek Mountain. The mountain is also called The Mountain that moved.

Prehistoric giant landslides extend for more than twenty miles along the eastern slope of Sinking Creek Mountain. These ancient landslides are the largest known landslides in eastern North America and are among the largest in the world. Some of the enormous slabs that have broken off are as big as 1.5 square miles in size. The slides were discovered in the 1980s during geological mapping. The Trail stretches across the benches of one of the slides.

Along the crest of Sinking Creek Mountain, you can see down the eastern slope toward Huckleberry Knob.

I saw two mountain goats as I was walking across the ridge. There were lots of deer tracks, but I did not see any deer. I can't believe the flowers, mountain laurels, and other vegetation growing out of the rocks.

We hiked through some thick patches of poison ivy. We immediately stopped and washed our legs off.

The rain cooled things off nicely so we are making good time. My sister does not like being up here.

We stopped at Niday Shelter for lunch and fresh water.

We finally made it into Catawba, Virginia and stayed at a private home we were told about. They will let you stay at no charge, but donations are welcome.

The accommodations were actually the garage of someone's house. They had cots and bales of hay set up for us to use. I am not sure if it is still open, so check the data books ahead of time. We went into town for dinner, and I finally had a great dinner of fried chicken and everything that went with it. We got a shower, but they did not have any laundry facilities. The owners were gracious enough to offer their computer and phone to anyone who needed to check their e-mail or call home. There were several people playing the guitar and just sitting around, catching up with each other. LaTripper and I set up our tents up on the hill, on a nice grassy spot. We hiked 15.9 miles today.

Saturday-I got some really bad news today. My sister is dropping off the trail. She told me it was one of the hardest decisions she has ever made. There was a lot of hugging and tears as she said good-bye to me and all our new friends. She was always worried about her daughter, Amber, who had never been on her own before. She was hoping to go home and check on her daughter and come back out on June 14, meeting me in Glasgow, Virginia.

I went out by myself today. I had a knot in my stomach, which could have been a little bit of fear and sadness of not having my hiking buddy to join me on my hike. I was going to wait and see my sister off to the bus station, but I knew if I waited, I would give in and go home with her. I was very tempted to call it quits. The idea of having a soft bed to sleep in and real food again was a very tempting alternative to going back out on the trail.

I got a ride to the trail. I was nervous on my first night alone, but I had my guardian angel watching over me. I met a group of Girl Scout moms who were out hiking by themselves. They were so interested in my hike so we sat for hours chatting about the trail and my adventures. They shared real food with me and gave me some brownies for the next day. They asked for my web site so they could follow my journey down the AT.

Clydesdale was at camp tonight. When I first met Grayson, Clydesdale and she were hiking together. He is hiking alone now and asked if I would like to hike with him up McAfee's Knob tomorrow. I told him I would love to have the company. Every time he is in town, he calls his wife to check his budget and modify his mail drops. He said he has not hiked with Grayson and had not heard from her for several days. It would be nice if I could catch up with her and have some companionship while out here. It's lonely without my sis. Sandman and Wrong Way showed up about 8:00 p.m. They pitched their tents near mine. I feel safe now and back in my element again. There are a lot of day hikers here today. This is probably the first time I was glad to have a crowd of campers nearby.

It was an easy hike today. I know now that I will be just fine, but I am still missing LaTripper.

I hiked 13.9 miles alone to the Catawba Mountain Shelter. I decided to set up my tent since the shelter was full.

Sunday-There are notices posted for the hikers alerting them of a very contagious stomach virus. I'm using extra precautions with the privy and personal hygiene.

Smoky dropped off, but his hiking partner, Yukon, is going on. She dropped off in Pearisburg but is thinking about coming back out for Shenandoah Day.

I started out at 7:00 a.m. this morning, which is the earliest I have ever left from camp. I ate my brownie that my new friend Dot gave me last night. It was a treat to have some goodies instead of my boring trail mix. I saw three deer this morning. They didn't seem to mind me hiking past. They stopped and watched me for a moment and then just continued eating.

The view at the top of McAfee's Knob is spectacular. Before you reach the summit, you pass through a section called the Devil's Kitchen, an area of huge flat-top boulders. It was such fun to wander through them. The mountain laurel is in full bloom up here. There are lizards everywhere just scurrying all over the rocks and taking in the sun. It is just a perfect setting and has helped my sadness change to a newly restored excitement to be hiking again. I would like to come back to this spot again and bring my sister back with me.

As tempting as it might be to camp up here, the data books informed us that it is forbidden to camp on the rocks. I did see a few who might have spent the night when I came through.

From McAfee's Knob, I climbed up to Tinker cliffs at three-thousand-foot elevation. On a clear day, you can see McAfee's Knob, which is where you just came from. We were lucky to have beautiful clear skies.

I stayed at the Best Western in Daleville for two nights. I shared the room and expenses with two other hikers. They were into partying with all the other hikers, but I chose to enjoy the cool air-conditioning and movies all day on the television. I don't think they will get out very early tomorrow. I spent Monday at the hotel and took care of all my errands and got lots of rest.

My total miles today were 17.6.

McAfee's Knob offers breathtaking, panoramic 270-degree views of the Catawba Valley. Look west and you can see the Allegheny Mountains, and if you look northeast, you will see Sharp Top Mountain.[5]

Tuesday—I was on the trail at 7:00 a.m. again today. My roommates partied until 1:00 a.m. and were still sleeping when I left. I've crossed three stiles in the first hour of my hike, and I am coming out of town with a full pack. It's warm and humid already this morning.

They predicted it would get up in the nineties today.

It's like a zoo out here with the squirrels, rabbits, turtles, and birds. They seem to be enjoying the heat of the morning more than I am.

I stopped at the Fullhardt Knob Shelter for a break and decided to push on for a few more miles. Jason was there with his dog. Jason has been at the shelters I have stopped at for several nights now. I love his dog. She does so well out on the trail. She carries her own food in a doggie backpack. He said he has had to slow down for his dog since it's been so hot.

The wild berries are slowly starting to get ripe. I have enjoyed a few.

I called my son Jeff, who lives in Idaho, to see if he had heard from Eddie. He said he had been there and left to go camping and prospecting for gold. This is the joy of his life, and I always enjoy going with him.

I couldn't go any farther than Wilson Creek Shelter with this heat. It wears me down until I have no energy left. Clydesdale is here again tonight. I think everyone else is pushing on to the next shelter.

I only hiked 11.2 miles today.

---

[5] Photographed by Bob Stimson and approved by ATC

Wednesday-I left at 6:30 so I could get a head start on the heat of the day, but it's already very hot and humid. There is a nice breeze though.

There have been daily sightings of timber rattlesnakes, but I haven't seen any yet. I stopped wearing my radio so I could hear the rattle of the snake if I came upon one.

I crossed the Blue Ridge Parkway at Black Horse Gap today. The trail parallels the Parkway, and later the Skyline Drive, for approximately two hundred miles. There is no hitchhiking allowed on the Parkway.

Most of the day has been ridge walking. It's nice not to be climbing all day. I have had great views from the ridge line.

I stopped at the Bobblets Gap Shelter for a break and to fill my water bottles. I've been hiking at times today with Baltimore Jack, Clydesdale, Jason and his dog, and Trip and her friend.

I stopped at Jennings Creek and decided to set up my tent by the river. I am leaving my rain cover off tonight so I can catch a breeze. As soon as I got to camp, I dropped my backpack and just jumped into the river to cool off. That's the next best thing to a good shower. We tried to catch a trout for dinner, but we didn't have any luck. We could hear deer all around our tents during the night. They made a snorting sound, and at first, I wasn't sure what they were, but the next morning, someone confirmed that it was indeed deer.

I have now completed one-third of the trail. I am even more motivated than ever to complete the trail. I hiked my first twenty-mile day today.

Thursday-I had a really good night's sleep and was up at 5:30 this morning. I was on the trail by 7:00 and starting climbing right away. I climbed two thousand feet right out of camp. I am tired today. I don't know if it's the heat, or I am coming down with something. I have several climbs today, and they are calling for thunderstorms tonight. I hate to get caught at the summit during a storm so I might take a short day. I wish I could get over my severe fear of lightning storms.

I stopped at Bryant Ridge Shelter for my morning break. This is one of the best shelters I have seen on the trail so far. It is a timber-frame shelter with three levels but limited tent sites.

There's a nice stream you cross just south of the shelter, which is a good source of water if you are not going to be stopping at the shelter. I seem to be finding better sources of water since I hit central Virginia.

The Queen Anne's lace and wild roses on top of Floyd Mountain are very impressive. Floyd Mountain is the highest climb today at 3,560 feet. The Queen Anne's lace stands five to six feet tall on this mountaintop.

Queen Anne's is a fern-like plant with elegant white lacy flowers

and has a long taproot, which, if dug up and crushed, smells just like carrots. They are also edible. This plant can be found almost anywhere in the world. It can become very aggressive and take over an entire field or roadside. You may find numerous names for this plant such as Bird's Nest Weed, Wild Carrot, Devil's Plaque, Fool's Parsley, and others.

The squirrels are more active, and they seem to be getting larger as we go farther north. The vegetation is so thick here. The volunteers have done a wonderful job keeping the trail cut back for us.

I feel like I'm in Georgia with all these ups and downs today. I went from one thousand feet up to two thousand feet the first thing this morning and then right back down to one thousand two hundred feet. I thought that was the last climb, but up we went again to 3,500 feet. The terrain was good without many rocks.

I decided to stop early at Cornelius Creek Shelter. I want to be on Apple Orchard Mountain early in the morning and hopefully see a beautiful sunrise. When I got into camp, several hikers were enjoying a break, and I thought the shelter might be busy tonight, but everyone decided to push on. I think I am going to be the only one here tonight.

I'm feeling sadness tonight. I miss LaTripper, Eddie, and my children. It's not good to stop so early; you have too much free time on your hands once you get all the camp chores done. I decided to play some good tunes on the radio and found a good country music station. It's now four thirty, and no one has shown up yet. I guess this will be my first night totally alone out here in the big bad woods. I started to feel edgy and unsettled, thinking about being in the woods alone. Music has always been good therapy for me, so I cranked it up, put my earphones on, got up on the picnic table, and started dancing. I swayed and I bumped and did a few country dances, the whole time keeping my eyes on the trail, worried someone might see me dancing up on the table. I went exploring around the shelter and found signs of deer in the area. Hopefully, I will see some in camp when it gets dusk. There is an unmarked trail behind the shelter one mile to a fire road and then left two-tenths of a mile to the Blue Ridge Parkway.

I am going to bed early so I can get up early tomorrow.

Friday-I made it! The buggy man or bears didn't get me in the middle of the night.

Again, I slept like a baby. I guess the extra miles I am hiking just wear me out. It looks like rain, but it's cooler than yesterday. Apple Orchard Falls is located about two and a half miles north of Cornelius Creek Shelter, down aside trail. I was told they were not flowing with the drought we are experiencing so I decided not to walk the additional three miles. I plan on coming back someday. I understand they are quite impressive.

I crossed, or was in sight of, the Blue Ridge Parkway at least five times today. I haven't seen much traffic, which surprises me since this is season for the Parkway.

My next climb took me to the top of Apple Orchard Mountain at an elevation of 4,225 feet. This is the highest mountain in central Virginia and the highest until you reach Mount Moosilauke in New Hampshire. Apple Orchard Mountain looks down on Peaks of Otter, Sharp Top, and Flat Top Mountains. On the climb up, it was raining, and the wind was blowing all the blossoms off the trees. The entire trail was covered with flower petals, and I felt like I was in a dream world. It was an amazing hike with the birds singing, colorful butterflies flitting all around me, misty air ferns swaying in the wind, and all the flower petals on the ground. Before you get to the top, you hike under the Guillotine, which is a large boulder over top of the trail between rock formations. I was so anxious to reach the top and take in the views I have read about, only to find it totally fogged in with no views at all. I will definitely come back to this area again.

I'm hiking alone, and I haven't seen many hikers today.

I love the beauty and solitude, but I do miss the human interaction. As the thru-hikers begin to drop off, they begin to get more spread out. I am missing some of the people I hiked with on and off in the early days.

This was once an Air Force radar base. The meadows were covered with barracks and support-service buildings for 250 people.

I've been reading reports in the shelters about a forest fire north of us. The name of the fire is Marble Yard, and 450 acres are on fire. They think lightning caused the fires. The smell of smoke is very unsettling. The rangers are going to reroute us ten miles around the fire area. This section could be closed for several weeks. The rangers met us at Petites Gap and shuttled us ten miles beyond, to the James River footbridge.

James River Footbridge

In 1991, Bill Foot proposed that the NBATC build a footbridge over the James River for the hikers. In order to receive grant money, he had to come up with supporters. He approached VA Department of Game and Inland Fisheries, VA Department of Conservation and Recreation, CSX Railroad, VA Department of Transportation, George Washington and Jefferson National Forests, ATC, and the NBATC.

Eventually, he was approved for one and a half million dollars if they could match 20% of these funds ($300,000). Nine years later, it all came together and the 650-foot bridge was completed. In the spring of 2000, Bill Foot died of cancer and never got to see the success of all his hard work. The bridge was dedicated on October 14, 2000 and named after Bill Foot.[6]

The rangers had cold drinks and snacks waiting for us. I talked to one ranger into taking me the six miles into Glasgow, Virginia. We would have crossed this six-hundred-foot bridge, which is for foot traffic only, if we had not been rerouted. I will come back at a later date to hike the ten miles I am going around. This section of the trail is located at US 501 and VA Route 130 at the James River. If not for Bill Foot, we would still be crossing a narrow two-lane highway, sharing it with logging trucks and other traffic, making it a very dangerous crossing.

I got a hotel and spent the night in Glasgow, Virginia. It's a small town, but it has all the amenities a hiker might need. Town can be so unsettling to your daily hike. It can suck you in and make you question why you're going back out. I was tempted until I called LaTripper and other family. She had heard about the fire and was very concerned about me. She was glad to hear from me but informed me she was not coming back out. I had prepared myself for this, but it still hurts to think I will attempt to complete the trail without my hiking buddy.

I completed 19.8 miles today. That includes the ten miles I was rerouted around.

---

[6] History of James River Bridge provided by ATC.

I left town with the smell of smoke in the air. I found this to be very unsettling.

Saturday-I walked the one mile out of town to the fork in the road and began hitchhiking the five miles to the trail. There was a lot of traffic, but no one was stopping. I have always prided myself in making the right choices based on my gut feelings. I had a car of three young guys go by, and shortly afterward, they came back. I did not feel good about my choice to go with them, but I did anyway. Only one of them spoke broken English, but he understood where I needed to get out. Everything worked out, but I learned my lesson: if it does not feel right, pass it up. When I got out, I got on the trail going south and waited for a while to turn around and go north.

I am seeing lots of wildlife today.

I had a lot of climbs again today but was more rested after a town night. The climb up Bluff Mountain was beautiful and worth it to arrive at a magnificent view. I could look back and see the smoke from the fire I had just gone around. I am so glad to be clear of the fear of that fire now. There is a memorial at the top for Little Ottie. In 1890, this was where they found his body after he wandered away from school. He was only four years old.

I stopped at Punch Bowl Shelter for a break and water and decided to continue another four miles to the Little Irish Creek. I was so glad I continued on to the creek. I met this really nice gentleman who was camping on the other side of the water in his van. He offered to share his campfire so two other hikers and I went over and sat around the fire for the evening. He said he had seen Grayson, who is one day ahead of me. It was nice to have my tent tucked into the woods away from everyone else. I fell asleep to the sounds of the water trickling over the rocks. I hiked 13.6 miles today.

Sunday-I heard deer roaming around outside of my tent last night.

I was the first hiker to break camp and head out so I am clearing the trail of all the cobwebs for the other hikers. I crossed under a dam, which was very eerie. As usual, the birds were singing to me as I hiked along. I did not wear my radio since I didn't want to miss the sounds of nature all around me. I put it on at night to catch up on the news and any weather issues and then I fall to sleep with some soft tunes.

I stopped at Brown Mountain Creek Shelter. I wish it were time to stop for the night. It is a beautiful setting. The tent sites are on the river. When I left the shelter, I walked along the river for the next mile. I loved the remoteness and the subtle beauty of the stream. The ruins I saw are from a community of freed slaves from the Civil War time until about 1918. Archaeological studies are still underway. The ruins have been visible for about one mile along the stream.

I met an eight-year-old girl named Alexandra, who was hiking with her dad. As we chatted, she was full of questions about my thru-hike attempt. She said she was going to do a thru-hike someday as well.

Today is Father's Day, and I have been thinking about Dad a lot and how much I miss him. I am so thankful to have had such supportive parents. I know they would be proud of my accomplishments and very supportive of my endeavor. I have always said that this hike is for me but in honor of my mom and dad. Their love of the outdoors and nature is the root of my being.

As I was coming through an absolutely peaceful part of the trail today, I was reminded of a poem Mom loved, titled "Trees." It has such meaning to me I have decided to add it for inspiration to anyone who loves nature as much as I do.

Trees

I THINK that I shall never see
A poem lovely as a tree
A tree whose hungry mouth is prest
Against the earth's sweet flowing breast;
A tree that looks at God all day,
And lifts her leafy arms to pray;
A tree that may in summer wear
A nest of robins in her hair;
Upon whose bosom snow has lain;
Who intimately lives with rain.
Poems are made by fools like me,
But only God can make a tree.   *Joyce Kilmer*

I will never forget my surprise as I came out of the woods at US 60 and began to cross the road to continue north. Grayson was just getting out of the car and saying good bye to her friend. She had gone home for a few days because of foot problems and her friend was just now dropping her off to continue her hike. I guess Grayson was feeling depressed, but she was determined to finish her hike. We would not have to hike alone anymore.

We hiked up Cold Mountain, which is another bald. I love the balds. NBATC and the Forest Service mow the bald to preserve the views and habitat for cottontail rabbits, various raptors, turkeys, and grouse.

Everyone is still behind us. I did not plan on doing a twenty-mile day, but Grayson did not want to stop so soon since she had just started out from where we met. Needless to say, my feet hurt tonight. I had five significant climbs today. The deer are everywhere now. I saw several on the way into camp. We hiked until 8:00 p.m. Water is a tenth of a mile north of shelter so we got water before setting up for the night.

Grayson and I pushed on to Seeley Woodworth Shelter after hiking a long 20.2 miles.

Monday-I left camp at eight forty-five alone. Grayson was still sleeping. She will catch up with me at the next shelter. I had a great night's sleep, and it is much cooler today.

I called my nephew Brian Schneider and asked him to change the dates on some of my mail drops since I am starting to hike more miles a day than I planned on.

While I was on Spy Rock, I saw several deer. They just kept eating but watching me as I watched them. Spy Rock is said to be the spot where Confederate soldiers used to spot activities of Union troops during the Civil War.

I'm entering the Priest Wilderness in the George Washington National Forest. In 2000, the United States Congress designated the Priest Wilderness, encompassing 5,963 acres of wilderness.

The trail has suddenly become very rocky. My feet feel battered. I stopped at the Priest Shelter for lunch to rest up from the hike up Priest Mountain. Grayson caught up with me there. We had a tortuous descent from four thousand feet down to one thousand feet in four and a half miles. It was very steep with a lot of loose rock. My feet are killing me.

There are only four in the shelter tonight. Grayson doesn't like to set up her tent. She likes the convenience of throwing down your sleeping bag, and you're ready to go. There is a group of Boy Scouts, but they are in their tents. We stopped at Harpers Creek Shelter and hiked 14.3 miles today.

Tuesday-The Humpback Rocks wore me out. Grayson kept saying there is no end; we are on the devil's treadmill. I didn't even take time to enjoy the views since I had to watch my footing most of the way. I wonder if this is the way the famous rocks of Pennsylvania will be.

It started out nice and cool, but it is very hot now. I think today is the worst day for me since I started my hike. We hopped from boulder to boulder or traversed on sharp rocky terrain all day. If that wasn't enough, everything was covered with poison ivy. There have been numerous sightings of rattlesnakes in this terrain, but so far, I have not seen any.

I saw a zebra long wing butterfly while sitting at the top of Glass Hollow Overlook. They have black wings with light yellow zebra-like stripes and long black antennae.

Zebra Longwing Butterfly

My mom taught us to always look for the good in the bad so here goes.

- I have Grayson as my hiking buddy to share my misery.
- It was only ninety degrees today instead of one hundred degrees.
- The sun was shining and it didn't rain, which would have caused the rocks to be treacherous.
- We made it safely into camp without an injury to our ankles.

Even when I have a bad day, I am still determined to continue on unless physically unable. Most days, I enjoy my hike and the great people I am meeting. I can't believe how hungry I am all the time. I'm going to get some protein drinks and talk with someone for ideas on food supplements to help me increase my energy.

Survivor is a section-hiker who had cancer and beat it so he hikes to stay fit. He started his hike while he was on treatment and found this was a way to help heal his body. He offered a prayer for Grayson and me to have a safe journey.

We have to hike 14.5 miles tomorrow so we can make it into Waynesboro. A friend of Grayson has invited us to her home when we reach the area.

We set up camp in the woods tonight. My feet, body, head, and everything else seem to hurt, so my day is done. We only hiked 12.7 miles today.

Wednesday-I'm seeing a lot of deer since I got to central Virginia. My wildlife sightings consisted of a groundhog, several rabbits, and two deer. I also had to chase a large black snake out of the trail.

On the way to Rockfish Gap, we passed through an old settlement with a cemetery that is said to be haunted. Uneventful day except for the time spent trying to track down Grayson's friends, Tammie and Paul. Paul's trail name was" Sharky". He is a successful thru-hiker, but I'm not sure what year he said he completed the trail. We hiked 14.6 miles today.

The trail comes out at US 250 and Interstate 64 in Rockfish Gap. I waited by the side of the road while Grayson trekked up to the hotel to see if she could reach Tammie. She was gone for some time when I heard thunder, and the threat of rain was very near. I had my pack and hers so I decided I better find cover before it started to rain. I made two trips to the visitor's center and sat a little bit longer to wait for Grayson. After a while, I became concerned so up the hill I went to track her down, only to be told she had already left and was heading back down. Off I went, and we finally connected at the visitor's center. Shortly after that, Paul showed up and brought us to his home in Waynesboro. What a beautiful home they have. They sit on acres of beautiful green meadows with a view of the Humpback Mountains we hiked yesterday. The hot tub is just what us weary hikers need to soothe our tired joints.

Grayson's friend Gail met us and spent the night with us. Tammie prepared us a wonderful dinner, and we enjoyed the evening just sharing trail stories. Tammie had been hiking with her daughter when she fell, spraining her ankle. This is where Grayson had met her on the trail and had stayed in touch with her.

The next morning, Gail took us to town, shopping at the mall. It was an enjoyable day just getting back to the real world for a short time. We decided to spend a second night and leave early the following morning.

Friday-We took a leisurely morning leaving for the trail. Paul drove us back to the trail after a big breakfast. Last night, Paul critiqued my backpack, at my request, to see if I could get my weight down at all. I ended up sending a few items home. It is always hard to get back into the routine of putting one foot in front of the other all day long.

The terrain was much easier today, but my energy was still low. There were several radar towers at the top of this small mountain we climbed coming out of Rockfish Gap, and they had tractor seats lined up for you to sit and enjoy the views or watch the skies at night.

We met Vernon Vernier, MD, who is known as DelDoc on the trail. He is walking the trail, surveying the whole AT with a GPS for the ATC and the NPS. He also did a survey of the trail in 1999. He has mapped 990 miles, which is 48 percent of the trail so far. He said that this is his fourth thru-hike. I found out later that he has an RV waiting for him whenever possible to spend the night in and refresh.

Vern was an ardent long-distance runner and hiker who was proud of taking part in twenty-seven marathons, including fourteen in Boston. He hiked the length of the AT nearly four times. Vern was the hiking medical columnist for the Appalachian Trailway News and wrote extensively, giving advice on nutrition, foot care, and general health to many hikers. Vern passed away in 2004.

Grayson saw her first bear today. I was directly behind her, but the bear was too fast so I didn't get to see it. There is a note in the shelter stating that six bears came into the area and ate someone's food. One of the hikers had to go back to Waynesboro and replenish his supplies. Jason and his dog, Carrigan, a group of Boy Scouts, Rob, and several other day hikers are at the shelter tonight. I'm glad Grayson and I aren't alone since there have been bear sightings in the area.

We only completed seven miles today and stopped at Calf Mountain Shelter.

Saturday-I did not see any bears last night, but another camper said one came into camp and was playing with his camp chair. We did have flying squirrels chewing on our food bags last night. I was lucky though and did not have any damage.

I left without Grayson again this morning. She wanted to sleep in and said she would catch up with me at the next shelter. I love the smells and sounds of the forest early in the morning. I found my first blueberries this morning. I only found a few ripe ones, but they were very tasty. I saw my first rattlesnake today. Jason was about to sit down on this rock for a break when his dog began barking. Just behind the rock was a rattler.

I hiked through a section of forest that had burned in 2000. I couldn't believe how quickly it restores itself.

Water is getting harder to find again. I have to carry more since it's about twelve miles in between sources. What we are finding is usually a good running spring. Most of the streams are dried up. I sent my filter home and thought I would try using iodine tablets for a while.

Our bear friends are always curious but so far not a threat.

The shelter is busy again tonight. I guess this time of year and weekends will continue to be a busy time. We had four in the shelter and six in their tents. I find I am setting up my tent more often. I am really bored with shelter life and all the snoring, mice all over the place, spiders, and hikers coming in late after I am in my sleeping bag sound asleep, and firing up the stove for the second dinner of the day. My tent is an escape from all this and my private space to wash up and write in my journal. My sister always liked to find a site away from a shelter near a bubbling brook. I think that was the only time she would get a good night's sleep. She has restless leg syndrome (RLS) and wakes up during the night numerous times.

I hiked thirteen miles alone today and stopped at Blackrock Hut. I really don't like hiking alone every day. I enjoy the camaraderie of a fellow hiker.

Blackrock Hut

SHENANDOAH NATIONAL PARK

HISTORY AND CULTURE IN THE PARK

June 24-28, 2002

The following information was taken from the US National Park Service's web site. This is a very extensive site and will provide you some wonderful information about the park.

The Europeans experienced the beauty of these mountains less than three hundred years ago. First came hunters and trappers, and soon after 1750, the first settlers moved into the lower hollows near springs and streams. Over the next century and a half, many hundreds of families built homesteads, mills, and stores and planted orchards and crops.

With the establishment of the park in December 1935, the Civilian Conservation Corps (CCC) began to build visitor facilities throughout the mountains. The beginning of WWII completed the core of the park's development.

APPALACHIAN TRAIL IN SHENANDOAH NATIONAL PARK

The Potomac Appalachian Trail Club (PATC) strongly supported the establishment of Shenandoah National Park, seeing the eastern national park as a means for the preservation of a large block of rustic, if not wilderness, land. The design and construction of the Skyline Drive between 1931 and 1939 caused a rift between the ATC and the PATC and the end of the friendship between MacKaye (founder of the AT) and PATC president Myron Avery. The Skyline Drive was being built on the crest of the Blue Ridge in the same location as the original AT. Most of the Trail had to be relocated and rebuilt lower down the mountain slopes. Avery believed that the roadway and the Trail could coexist and provide a recreational experience to great numbers of visitors, while MacKaye was unwilling to compromise with the automobile. He left the ATC and went on to found the Wilderness Society.

From 1933-1942, the CCC built the new Trail and structures associated with the AT, but then and today, the PATC administered the Trail cabins and huts and partnered with the National Park Service in maintaining the route. Today, 101 miles of the Appalachian Trail wind their way through the park. The forest has changed since 1926, and the Trail has been shifted in places due to floods, fire, and landslides. However, the experience first sought by the early Trailblazers remains unchanged.

Shenandoah National Park has one of the densest populations of black bears documented within the United States. You might be lucky enough to spot white-tailed deer, gray squirrels, big brown bats, or a skunk. There are more than fifty species of mammals in the Park. There are occasional sightings of cougars and bobcats.

There are two hundred species of resident and transient birds in the park. Just a few you might see are the downy woodpecker, scarlet tanager, red tail hawk, Carolina chickadee, and wild turkey.

There are 862 species of wildflowers in the park. Hepatica is usually the first native wildflower to bloom in the spring in the park. These beautiful flowers are pink, six-petal flowers that fill the valley floors and hillsides.

Monday-I am really having a hard time with the heat and humidity. I left camp at eight, and it was already very hot. I think I need to start hiking at six and take a long break during the hottest part of the day. The smoke from the forest fire was very heavy this morning.

I'm feeling gloomy and sad that I haven't heard from my kids or friends for a while. I feel like they are involved with their everyday life and have forgotten about my day-to-day struggles out here. Hopefully, they are following my journal online at Trail Journals. Everyone's e-mails mean so much to me. They keep me motivated and lift me up when I am having my down days. Not every day out here is good, but most days, I am with my new circle of friends, and life is so very good. I am almost halfway to completing the entire trail.

We met a wonderful lady, Annie Kiermaier, who is hiking for one week to see if she wants to attempt a thru-hike in the near future. She hiked with us most of the day. She spent the night with us at camp and will hike with us tomorrow.

We are tired and stopped at the South River Picnic Grounds. There is no camping allowed here, but we are going to cook, use the picnic facilities, then sneak into the woods and set up camp. Hopefully, the rangers won't catch us and make us move in the middle of the night. The bugs are so bad I had to wear my mosquito netting to fix my dinner. I am set up, ready for bed, since the bugs are eating me alive, and am in my tent but hungry again with my food already hung in the tree. I guess I will go to sleep with an empty stomach. I heard a pack of coyotes during the night.

We hiked for 13 miles today.

Tuesday-As usual, it was very hot and humid already at 7:00 a.m. I was on the trail by seven thirty. I just don't seem to be able to get out any earlier especially if I am in my tent at night. Grayson and I left together today.

I saw my first bear. She was about twenty feet to the right of the trail. She stood up in the dense bushes on her hind legs and just watched me for a few moments. She didn't seem to be threatened so I watched for a few minutes. I clicked my poles together, and eventually, she meandered down the hillside. Everyone said I was lucky since normally, all you see is the rear end as they are on the run. I was not as fearful as I thought I might be.

I took a hard fall today. There were three of us with me in the lead. Since I was in front, I was catching all the spider webs in the face.

I decided to wave my poles back and forth to clear the way when I tripped on a rock and fell. It is only a matter of seconds, and you don't have time to react. I scraped my knee and elbow but came close to doing a touchdown with my nose and the trail. I caught my left cheek on a rock and had a significant-sized goose egg all day. I could sympathize with my sister now.

We took a break at Lewis Mountain campground for a couple of hours to cool off and get some refreshment. Annie decided she did not want to continue on with us.

With the heat, Annie is having a hard time keeping up with us and felt she was pushing herself too hard. She suggested that we stop at Big Meadows campground tomorrow and stay the night with her friends who are waiting for her to complete her few days out on the trail.

Annie Kiermaier and I stayed in touch, and I found out that she lives in Rockland, Maine, which is where we go in the summers. I called her and had dinner with her and her friend. I found out later that she had done a hike on the AT in the White Mountains and had a serious accident. She had been hiking alone and slipped on some ice, falling down the side of the mountain. She could not get out for two days and one night. She was on a small ledge and could not open her tent so she slept inside her bag and tent to keep warm. She finally was able to get out and hobbled down the trail to a ranger station for help. She ended up being flown out with several broken ribs and multiple contusions. After many months of healing, she was able to meet her friends when they reached North Carolina.

We pushed as far as Meadows campground and accepted Annie's offer to look up her friends. We were welcomed with open arms and pitched our tents next to theirs. Lucy ran us up to the store and the shower house. We joined them for dinner and had some real food for a change from our wonderful trail food.

For several days now, the heat and the bugs have been unbearable. My legs are covered with bug bites. There are so many restaurants and campgrounds in the park. If we decided to stop at all of them, we would never get out of the park. I am very tired, and my knee is bothering me so I guess I will call it a night.

We have hiked fourteen miles today.

Wednesday-I had a very restful night's sleep but did not get on the trail until 9:00 a.m. Lucy offered us some fresh fruit for our breakfast. We don't see fresh fruits or vegetables out here. It's much cooler so I am in a better frame of mind. As I left camp this morning, I saw five deer. We are making good time even with a late start. We heard thunder in the distance, and by the look of the sky, rain is moving in fast. We picked up speed to try and make it to the restaurant before it broke. We made it, but the sky became very dark while we were eating.

We treated ourselves to a wonderful lunch at the Skyland Lodge and Restaurant. Once we get through the Shenandoah Mountains, we won't have the opportunities to stop for lunch or dinner, so we will enjoy and not worry about the added expense. I had chicken potpie and blackberry cobbler with blackberry ice cream on top. The lodge has such beautiful views. I would love to come back and stay here in the future. The view from the restaurant is of the town of Luray and the valley beyond.

We decided to head out since the storm appeared to be heading in the opposite direction. We began to climb Stony Man Mountain, with an elevation of 3,800 feet, and were almost to the summit when the storm broke. My friends and family all know that my greatest fear, coming out here, was the lightning storms. I knew I had to get away from the tallest trees, but there was no time to get to a lower area. I took my tent's ground cover. Grayson and I climbed up onto a downed dead tree, back to back, underneath some small pines, and covered up to wait out the storm.

We were off hiking again, nice and dry, half an hour later. I was quite nervous during the storm but proud that I mastered my first big storm safely.

I followed several deer up the trail. They wanted to get around us but didn't know how since we were on a very rocky section with a steep drop-off. They finally made it.

We're not allowed to camp at Pinnacles Picnic area, but we will tuck back into the woods out of sight. The bugs are still really heavy, and I am wearing my mosquito netting again to prepare my supper and while I set up my tent. We had a magnificent sunset tonight with such a beautiful array of pinks. The valley below is splendid with the fluffy clouds settled into its folds.

We completed 12.3 miles.

Thursday-On our way out of camp, we saw eight deer.

Shenandoah National Park had their largest forest fire ever in the year 2000. They said it started in the Pinnacles Picnic Area. We have seen damage for more than two mountain ranges since we left camp.

Walking the trail is like driving from one vista or overlook to another. The underbrush is so thick in this area you can barely see the trail. It has acres of ferns, waist-high and very aromatic.

This fern is called the sweet fern and smells like you're traversing through a valley of aromatic flowers instead of ferns.

I saw such a variety of wildflowers today. I can't identify most of them, but I certainly will bring a book on flowers and birds next time I hike this area.

Grayson and I felt like we were in a magical jungle, and the next thing I knew, we were belting out the song "George of the Jungle."

Every mountain we climb is so unique in its own way. The vegetation, the views, and the wildlife change with each new climb. We crossed US 211 at Thorton Gap and saw a sign that said eight miles to

Luray. As a child, I remember my dad taking us to the Luray Caverns. If you have the chance to go, I think they are some of the most beautiful caverns I have ever seen.

While I was listening to my radio today, the song "Ain't Going Down Till the Sun Comes Up" came on. Ed and I like country dancing, and when we are in Florida, we go dancing every week. This is the song that my friend Karen and I dance the "Slap Leather" to. I stopped in the middle of the trail and started dancing. You can only imagine the scene. I was dancing with a forty-pound pack on my back, two hiking poles, hiking boots, a red hat, a pair of shorts that are now three sizes too big, and a black knee brace. What a Kodak moment I missed. Life is so very good.

I saw another bear today. We had just reached the summit of Hogback Mountain, with me in the lead, when I came around the bend and saw a large, five- or six-hundred-pound bear in the middle of the trail. He was heading north up the trail and probably only ten feet away from me. He looked over his shoulder and watched me for a moment. I slowly backed up around the bend, out of sight, and told Grayson there was a bear up ahead. She went on ahead, but by the time she got there, the bear was gone. It's amazing he could disappear that quickly since it was a sheer drop on the left and straight up on the right.

We outran another storm by five minutes and stopped at Elkwallow Gap Grill for a cheeseburger and fries while we waited out the storm. I am so glad we made it in time because it was a really bad one. The good part is it has cooled down nicely. We were able to hike until 8:00 p.m. It was a long day with lots of miles, numerous climbs, and storms, but my energy is good today. We are camping legally tonight in the Gravel Springs Hut. The spring is almost dried up. I hope we don't start having trouble getting water again. There is a family from Canada camping here tonight. They said there is still snow on Katahdin.

We had a 19.6-mile day.

Friday-We got a late start today. We are both worn out from our long day yesterday.

I am seeing the most beautiful yellow flowers. The flower has five petals and has blooms going up the stem. The plant stands about two feet tall and is called the yellow loosestrife.

We hit the trail at 10:00 a.m., but it felt good to sleep in. We slept in the shelter last night and did not have many bugs to contend with. There were only three in the shelter. This is a big change from the early days on the trail. I'm still not seeing many thru-hikers during the day. We are all quite spread out now. Hopefully, we will see most of our new trail friends in Harpers Ferry, West Virginia.

We are starting to find ripe blueberries and red raspberries. I lose a lot of time hiking because I stop and eat each time I find a new patch.

Shutter Bug noted in the register at the last shelter that he had a bear encounter. The bear was in the trail and would not move on so he hissed at it. He should have known better because the bear started coming toward him. He ducked behind a tree, and the bear finally moved on, growling as it went by.

I found that every mountain summit offered magnificent views of the valley below, and the climbs were gentle in comparison to what we have been climbing. The wildlife is so much more abundant than any forest we have been through. I have seen two bears, at least twenty deer, rabbits, groundhogs, grouse, wild turkey, squirrels, chipmunks, rattlesnakes, black snakes, many varieties of birds, and so many flowers, I can't even identify all of them.

We have had the opportunity every day to stop at a café for a break from trail food if we wanted to. My advice to anyone hiking this area is to slow down and enjoy what nature has to offer.

We made it to Tom Floyd Wayside Shelter and prepared to fetch water, which is usually the first thing I do when I get into camp.

The sign said two-tenths of a mile to the spring, which was probably half a mile straight down. The spring was running so slow the only water we could find was what was dripping from the pipe. It took me twenty minutes to fill one liter of water. I needed to fill two liters and a pan full to cook with tonight. Finally, after filling all my containers, I began the hike back up with two bottles, a pan of water, and one hiking pole. I had my camp shoes on already so hiking up was difficult. I am thankful that we were able to get water since I was out.

I can't believe how much stronger I have become out here. I am not just physically stronger, though my endurance and stamina have increased; it's my mental strength and confidence to be alone in such a challenging environment. I have far exceeded my expectations of life on the trail and all the trials we encounter every day. I have overcome so many fears of being alone in the wilderness, even though you are never really alone this time of year.

We did a short day today and are now outside of Shenandoah National Park. We arrived at camp at four in the afternoon since we only hiked for five hours, completing 10.5 miles.

Songs of Innocence Night

> *The sun descending in the west,*
> *The evening star does shine.*
> *The birds are silent in their nest,*
> *And I must seek for mine.*
> *The moon like a flower,*
> *In heaven's high bower,*
> *With silent delight*
> *Sits and smiles on the night.*　　　　　*William Blake*

NORTHERN VIRGINIA

June 29-July 2, 2002

The northern Virginia section stretches fifty-four miles from the Virginia and West Virginia line south to Shenandoah National Park.

Saturday-What a day! I can't believe how the forest changes when you leave Shenandoah National Park. The vegetation is so thick and dense you can't see where the trail is.

I found several ticks on me today. I found out from my sister that she acquired Lyme disease while she was out on the trail and started having symptoms shortly after she dropped off the trail.

> Deer ticks are one of the main carriers of Lyme disease. You should check yourself each night before you go to bed. In most cases, if you find a tick, you won't become infected. They usually need to be attached for thirty-six hours or longer to infect you.

Symptoms range from a red rash that spreads at the site of the bite, flu-like symptoms, extreme fatigue, headaches, sore muscles and joints, and fever. You should seek medical attention as soon as possible. If the bite is left untreated, you could develop skin problems, joint pain, and nervous system and heart problems. It may take weeks, months, or even years before these symptoms show up.

We came upon a tree that was down across the trail. We had to squeeze under it since it was too large to go over. I had to remove my pack to get under and crawl through the branches, pulling my pack along with me. I notified the volunteer who was working on the trail, and he said he would go back with a chain saw and remove it.

We really appreciate what the volunteers do for us out here. I don't think you would be able to get through the thick undergrowth and all the blow downs if they did not keep it cut.

There are a lot of wild strawberries along the trail, but they don't have much taste.

Grayson is meeting her friend in Harpers Ferry on July third so we are pushing miles. I would like to slow down while it's so hot, but I would like to be home for the fourth of July also. Eddie is going to meet me there if he can.

We stopped at Jim and Molly Denton Shelter for a break. They have a solar shower, which we took advantage of. It was cold, but it sure felt good after all the hot weather we have been having. The shelter has a patio with furniture and a separate pavilion with a table for cooking.

Beech said he had pitched his tent near where we stopped last night. He was walking along, and all of a sudden, a bear stood up out of the thick underbrush. They watched each other for a few seconds when all of a sudden, he saw two tiny cubs pop up. They all took off, but Beech was able to snap a quick photo.

We passed the National Zoological Research Center, which runs adjacent to US 522. We could not see anything through the fences, which went on for miles. I was told it is a home for rare endangered animals from all over the world. It was formerly a military reservation. The buildings and the land cover thousands of acres.

We had planned to hike the one mile into Linden, Virginia but decided to hike the additional two and a half miles to the shelter for the night. Our food supply is getting low, but we will try to make it to Ashby Gap and restock tomorrow. I've been told that you can get fresh-baked pies at the Apple House, but we were told at camp last night that they were out of pies.

Some hikers told us not to stay at Manassas Gap Shelter, that the shelter and the grounds were infested with copperheads. Someone killed a copperhead today, and one of the volunteers removed it. We decided to set up our tents off the trail before you exit down the side trail to the shelter. The only thing is, you have to go down to the shelter and beyond for your water source. I didn't like it but had to go twice to fill up my water bottles. The register in the shelter said a copperhead bit a dog about one mile south of the shelter. He stayed two nights at the shelter to allow his dog to heal. His foot swelled up very large but was normal in two days and seemed to be fine. It's going to be a long day tomorrow, so I'm going to bed early tonight. I'm listening to my tunes and trying to get to sleep. Ed, if you're reading my journal, I know you are on your way back east and probably looking up at the same sky and stars tonight that I am. I only hope that you are missing me as much as I am missing you. I'll see you soon, and I love you so much.

We hiked 13.6 miles today.

Sunday-We had nice terrain and good weather today. We seemed to walk for miles through grape arbors and blackberry bushes. I ate berries all day and picked some for breakfast tomorrow. We found a resting bench at the trailhead for Sky Meadows State Park. We rested there while we picked lots of red raspberries. While we were sitting there, a couple came up to us and wanted to hear all about our adventure and plans to complete the entire trail. They were from Chevy Chase, Maryland, which is not far from where I grew up.

We went into Ashby Gap to find some supplies but did not have much luck. We did find some cold Gatorade, which I crave when I hit a town. We indulged and had some ice cream as well.

Bryan, whose trail name is Lost and Found, is back on the trail. I've been reading his entries in the shelter registers. I think he is two days ahead of us.

I couldn't sleep so I was thinking about all the goals I have met so far. First, I have been on the trail for ninety-six days and have completed 973 miles. Second, I have been living in the woods for three months and six days. Third, I have completed almost four of the fourteen states so far.

We stopped at Rod Hollow Shelter after 13.4 miles.

Monday-Right out of the shelter this morning, we began the notorious roller coaster. In northern Virginia, the AT follows a long, low ridge. I hiked over the roller coaster, over thirteen miles of ups and downs over ten mountain ridges, all while hiking on rocks, then in the middle of it, they throw in the Devil's Racecourse, a short section over bigger rocks. The climbs averaged nearly five hundred feet up and down for each hill.

There are no views at the top, and the terrain can be quite rocky at times. Of course, it was extremely hot the entire day. Our only water source was a muddy puddle where a stream should have been. I am going to get my water filter back when I go home. The spring at Sam Moore Shelter was dried up.

We stopped at a remarkable place for the night called Bears Den Hostel, which is owned by the ATC and operated by the PATC. It was built around 1930 and transformed into a twenty-six-bed hostel. They have a small store that sells supplies and Ben & Jerry's ice cream. I paid $11.00 for a bunk with sheets, blanket, and pillow. This included full use of the upstairs kitchen. They let you work for your stay if you are short of funds. They also have a washer, dryer, and a large sitting room. The building is constructed of stone, and the grounds have a beautiful stone wall around the property. You can take a short walk to Bears Den Rock and enjoy the views at sunset.

We did 9.9 miles today and will finish up tomorrow.

Tuesday-We had blackberry pancakes and fresh fruit for breakfast.

Hot! Hot! I had a very hard time with the heat again. We were going to push on to Harpers Ferry, but neither of us had the energy.

We had an awesome view from Crescent Rock and Pulpit Rock. It was fun watching a group of young kids learning to rock-climb.

When I was doing my preparation hikes, I stayed at David Lesser Memorial Shelter with my sister. I have fond memories of us sitting with the other hikers, playing cards and drinking wine. I am sleeping with my rain fly off tonight. We stopped at David Lesser Memorial Shelter after hiking 11.1 miles.

David Lesser Memorial Shelter

Bear's Den Hostel

WEST VIRGINIA

July 3-6, 2002

You are only in West Virginia for two miles.

Wednesday's forecast spoke of temperatures in the upper nineties with a heat index of 105 degrees.

Beech has been hiking with us the last few days, but Frank is still behind us. No one has heard from him for several days.

Shortly after coming out of the woods, we crossed the Shenandoah River along US 340. It is about twenty miles east from the home where I grew up.

We made it to Harpers Ferry by ten thirty, and Ed was already waiting for me with his friend Ron. He said he drove until 3:00 a.m. to make sure he wasn't late. We gave Grayson a ride to the hotel where her friend was waiting. Ed and I then went to ATC headquarters. If you make it halfway, the ATC will take your photo and display it in that year's album. It was such fun to look and see if any of our friends had made it through yet. You can get Coleman fuel or alcohol for a donation. You can also have packages mailed to this address: ATC, PO Box 807, Harpers Ferry, West Virginia 25425.

This is the halfway mark. I am so excited to have made it halfway. We will reach the actual halfway marker further north.

Harpers Ferry holds a lot of memories for me. I grew up in Maryland, and every summer my dad would pack a picnic and let us play in the rivers. Afterward, we would tour the town, and my dad would share the Civil War history with us. My dad loved to study Civil War history. Maryland and the surrounding areas are so rich in history. Every time we would get company, my dad would take them to Gettysburg, Pennsylvania and Harpers Ferry to share the history of the area with them.

The hike up to Jefferson Rock is worth the extra miles. You will have an extraordinary view of the water gap, where the Potomac and Shenandoah Rivers meet. Another great hike is up Maryland Heights. I have done this with my sisters before. You are looking down on Harpers Ferry from up there.

You can get the Amtrak train from here to Washington, DC with previous reservations. Check the data book for days, time, phone numbers, and any updates on schedules.

From Harpers Ferry, I am going home for a couple of days and will head out again on Saturday.

We only hiked 8.6 miles.

On Thursday, July fourth, we had a family get-together at my sister's house. All my brothers and sisters were there. LaTripper and I did lots of catching up. Grayson and her friend Lois joined us. This is the first I have been home and seen any of my family in three months. It felt good to sleep in a real bed and eat real food.

It's hard to go home and settle in to the real world and then pack up and go back out on the trail. Every time I stop for a day or more, I am tempted to go home. I came very close to giving it all up. If Grayson had not been with me, I probably would have.

    We always enjoyed setting up camp at the end of the day by a bubbling brook. The power of the water rushing over the rocks is like a lullaby lulling us to sleep. It is so exciting to wake in the morning to such a serene setting with the sounds of rushing water, singing of the birds and the forest smell in the air. I am instantly refreshed and ready to tackle another day.

    Anticipate your day! I wish I could know the places I have yet to go, the ways I'll get there, the things I'll do, the special dreams I'll make come true. I wish I could see the life that lies ahead of me on my way to Katahdin.
    If I say yes to life by always laughing as much as possible and crying as little as possible I will conceive the inconceivable. Are you saying yes to life?

MARYLAND

July 7-9, 2002

The Appalachian Trail in Maryland follows a forty-one-mile route along the backbone of South Mountain, a north-south ridge that extends from Pennsylvania to the Potomac River. This section is great for three- or four-day trips, is easy by AT standards, and is a good place to find out if you're ready for more rugged parts of the trail. You are required to stay at designated shelters and campsites.

There are many pretty views and convenient access from nearby towns and highways. It's also a favorite with Scouts seeking the merit badge for a fifty-mile hike. Elevation changes are 230 to 1,800 feet. The black-capped chickadee is the state bird, and the black-eyed Susan is the state flower.

This is my home state.

Saturday-We're back on the trail after having two days off. Ed is heading for Maine for the summer, so I won't see him until I reach Maine, and Ron is heading back to Florida.

I have a full pack with six days of food. I have to carry more food to keep me nourished now. Sometimes my hunger overwhelms me. We are burning about five thousand calories a day. I have no body fat to fall back on, so I eat nonstop all day. My feet are hurting, but I will toughen them up real soon.

Nice cool breeze today. We crossed the Potomac River on a six-hundred-foot bridge that is the West Virginia and Maryland state line. We then followed the Chesapeake & Ohio (C&O) canal towpath for about three miles.

We stopped at Ed Garvey Shelter for lunch but did not get water here since it was down a steep, half-mile trail. We knew we could get water two miles north, at Gathland State Park.

I went through the museum at the park and spoke with two historians about the area. They offer interpretive programs throughout the summer featuring Civil War reenactments. On the trail is a large stone monument dedicated to the war correspondents.

The shelter is busy tonight. I decided to pitch my tent since Grayson found a snakeskin in the shelter. I kept expecting a visitor during the night. I have now hiked over one thousand miles of the Appalachian Trail.

We completed 11.1 miles and stopped for the night at the Crampton Gap Shelter.

> George Washington was one of the early proponents of a canal and reportedly rode his horse down what is now the C&O towpath. The canal was built in the 1830s. Using the towpath, mules pulled barges that were filled with goods headed for the frontier.
>
> Gathland State Park stands atop South Mountain, at Crampton's Gap, which is one of the three gaps involved in the battle of South Mountain on September 14, 1862, three days before the battle of Antietam.

Sunday-It's so good to be in my home state of Maryland. There is so much Civil War history here. I feel as if I am walking in the footsteps of our forefathers.

We stopped at Dahlgren Backpack Campground for a break. I was so excited to see hot showers for free. I don't know why I did not stop for a shower, but I did decline. I did take time to pick some red raspberries, fill my water bottles, and enjoy a break on the bench.

I'm seeing a lot of deer, but they don't seem to be as friendly as they were in Shenandoah Park.

My stove quit working just before I went home, but the guys worked on it, and it works perfectly now.

I have completed five states—Georgia, North Carolina, Tennessee, Virginia, West Virginia—and will complete Maryland tomorrow.

We passed the Old South Mountain Inn. I wonder if we smelly hikers would be welcome.

I read in the register that a hiker was struck by lightning on June 28 at Annapolis Rock. It was about five forty-five in the afternoon, and he walked halfway down, met a ranger, and was transported to the hospital.

We passed the stone Washington Monument, in Washington Monument State Park, that was built on South Mountain near Boonsboro, Maryland.

The citizens of the town built it. It is believed to be the earliest monument erected in honor of the country's first president, George Washington. It was dedicated on July 4, 1827. During the Maryland campaign of 1862, the monument was used as a signal tower. Five hundred townspeople erected fifteen feet of the monument by four in the afternoon on the first day. This was on a fifty-four-foot circular base. You can climb up to the observation deck and enjoy the view of the surrounding country.

We crossed US 40 at Greenbrier State Park after crossing a footbridge over Interstate 70.

There is only one in the shelter tonight. Grayson and I are the only ones sleeping in our tents. It was a nice spot except for the traffic sounds from I-70. We hiked 12.5 miles and stopped at Pine Knob Shelter.

I came to a plaque along the trail that posted the following battle during the Civil War.

It was on this spot, on September 4, 1862, that Stonewalls regiment, the 17th Michigan Volunteer Infantry, engaged in battle. Fighting began at 9:00 a.m. and at 4:00 p.m., the command was given for an assault along the entire Union line of five hundred men of the Stonewall regiment. Twenty-seven were killed and 114 wounded many mortally."

Monday-We hiked up to Annapolis Rock this morning and enjoyed the views of Greenbrier Lake and Cumberland Valley. We also went up to Black Rock Cliffs. These are some of the best views we have had in quite a while.

Rob Silver Feet, the Maryland ridge runner, wrote in the registry, "Be who you seek to be, one moment, one breath, one step at a time." That's what I'm talking about!

We are starting to find lots of rock along the trail. I was hoping they would wait until we got into Pennsylvania. The Maryland that I grew up in is more rolling hills with lots of farmland.

I tripped and hit my face on a rock along the trail again today. I must say my black eye may be blacker than LaTripper's was.

We stopped at Penn Mar County Park for a cheeseburger and ice cream. We had fantastic views of Waynesboro, Smithfield, and Hagerstown. We had a nice breeze all day, and it's a bit cooler. We crossed into Pennsylvania at the Mason-Dixon Line.

We have completed six states and have eight more to go. We are not far from Camp David, I was told. We hiked through the "devil's racecourse" today. It's a field of boulders that you have to climb up, down, around, and at the same time, try to find a blaze to make sure you are still on the AT. There were rocks and boulders as far as you could see.

My pack feels so heavy since I came back out. I keep kidding Grayson that she put rocks in it when I wasn't watching. We found a spot in the woods around 8:00 p.m. and retired early. We hiked seventeen miles.

PENNSYLVANIA

July 10-26, 2002

The trail in Pennsylvania follows ridges of mountains east of the Alleghenies to the Susquehanna River in a long section of trail notorious for its foot-bruising rocks. If your feet hold up for the next rock-pounding 232 miles, the rest is just a walk in the woods.

The state flower is the mountain laurel, and the state bird is the ruffed grouse.

The trail north of the Susquehanna is characterized by long, flat, rocky ridges broken by fairly strenuous climbs in and out of gaps.

About ten miles south of the Susquehanna River, the trail crosses the great valley of the Appalachians to the Blue Ridge. This southern portion of the trail through Pennsylvania has many sections that are gentle, and grades are easy, making it one of the easiest sections of the trail. The trail passes many roads through this section, and some shelters are near roads. You can expect elevation changes from 320 to 2,080 feet. There are 229 AT miles in Pennsylvania.

Tuesday-Ruby and her dog, Jane, have been hiking with us on and off since we left Damascus. Jane and three other puppies had been abandoned, and they were trying to find them homes when Ruby came along and adopted one. Jane has adapted to trail life very well.

All the shelters in Pennsylvania are double shelters. We stopped at the Antietam Shelter, soaked our feet in the stream, and had a much-needed rest. I wish I could find a stream like this at the end of each day.

We seem to be crossing a road almost every hour today, but town is not easily accessible from most of the road crossings.

We had a challenging climb today. We went straight up for one thousand feet to Chimney Rocks.

Chimney Rocks is a natural geological formation on Catfish Mountain. These are limestone formations containing 120 perches. You can sit in Chief's Seat, which is a rock pad atop the limestone pillars. In 1994, the Borough of Hollidaysburg, PA, purchased Chimney Rocks.

We continued climbing up to 1,900 feet in 1.3 miles. We decided to pass Rocky Mountain Shelter and push forward to Caledonia State Park. Imagine our surprise to get to the bottom and find two coolers with cold drinks and a note that said the first eight hikers were welcome to set up at spots ninety-seven and ninety-nine. We hiked thought the park to check it out. Just as we got there, it began raining.

They served us barbecued ribs, potatoes, green beans, and fresh fruit. They are also going to cook us a big breakfast. Scott, a previous thru-hiker, is funding the whole week and trying to look out for the weary hikers. He made two trips to Wal-Mart for anyone who needed supplies. We did not go but put in an order for ice cream. I ate a pint in one sitting. He does this every year as long as he can fund the venture. I wish I could find true friends like this in the real world. This type of kindness is so hard to find in my normal life. They truly and sincerely care about us out here.

My feet are really beginning to bother me. I didn't realize how bruised I was from my fall until I took my shower. I have four bruises on my shoulder, one on my hip, a black eye, and a swollen and bruised left cheek. It's still raining so I guess I will call it a night.

We hiked 18.3 miles.

I have always been fascinated by Caledonia and the history of this area. Wesley R. Foltz from Shippensburg University gave me the following information on this area.

> This area is rich with Civil War history. Thaddeus Stevens chose to build his Caledonia Ironworks here for the production of horseshoes, hinges, wagon wheels, and other assorted tools. All of these products could then be transported east or west on what would become known as the Lincoln Highway.
>
> During the 1830s and 1840s, Thaddeus fended off bankruptcy and sought money to keep his struggling Caledonia Ironworks afloat, in large part because they and the surrounding twenty thousand acres that he owned were conduits for the Underground Railroad, in addition to being the region's largest employers of African American workers. An estimated forty thousand

to sixty thousand slaves successfully escaped into freedom.

The cottage that is rented to the public was the Caledonia Furnace Store and is the only structure certain to have dated to the Civil War. It is a log structure with two-hundred-year-old white oak beams now resting on 1950s-era concrete blocks.

Wednesday-While I was packing up to leave camp, I felt my finger crack, and it became very painful. Scott, our host, is an EMT so he looked at it and agreed it was probably broken. He splinted it and taped my two fingers together.

This was an easy section of trail. We seem to be crossing roads all day. It was much cooler today, and the terrain was much easier so we took our time. We stayed at Toms Run Shelters and hiked 16.4 miles today. This is a double shelter and will sleep up to eight in each shelter.

Thursday-We caught up with Tweety today at Pine Grove Furnace State Park. She had taken some time off to let her leg heal. Now we are the three musketeers. She had spent the night here at the hostel and was about to leave when she saw us. She started to cry, and there were hugs all around. She was feeling very lonely hiking by herself and was so glad to catch up with us. I know the feeling. The hostel closed at 9:00 a.m. so we were not able to shower or do our laundry as we had planned.

You should plan on stopping here for a short break and join the half-gallon club. All you have to do is eat a half-gallon of ice cream to celebrate having made it halfway along the trail. With relocations, the true halfway point of the trail is now about a half mile south of PA 233. Grayson and Tweety decided to try for the award but did not quite make it through the whole box. One hiker ate his half-gallon and decided to try for another. He ended up using the trashcan that was next to him. I wouldn't want to start hiking with a belly full of ice cream in this heat.

While passing through Pine Grove today, we saw the historic furnace that was used to smelt iron during the Civil and Revolutionary Wars.

Friday-Last night was perfect at fifty degrees, and we were on the trail by 8:00 a.m. It was an easy hike up to our first overlook. We sat at the top, on the rocks, having a snack and enjoying the view of the ridge on the other side. It was a very peaceful spot. The sky was such a pretty blue with wispy clouds running through it. As we were sitting and enjoying the moment, we realized that there weren't any birds singing.

I really enjoy hiking with Grayson and Tweety. We made it into Boiling Springs earlier than expected. The trail passes by the ATC Mid-Atlantic Regional Office. This is a good place to stop for trail updates and weather reports. We decided to stay at Garmanhaus B&B. They will let you pitch a tent in their backyard for a small fee, and for two dollars, they will do your laundry for you. There are no shower facilities, but we walked down the road to the swimming pool.

We hiked 12.2 miles today.

Boiling Springs is called the Children's Lake and is dedicated to our children's children. The lake is a seven-acre lake dating back to 1750, when it was dammed to power the ironworks. It is fed by some thirty natural springs that bubble up to the surface from subterranean caves, estimated to be 1,800 feet below the surface. They deliver about twenty-two million gallons of crystal-clear, fifty-three-degree water per day. Recently, people have started scuba diving and going down in the lake's caves.

Saturday-My energy is very low today. We left Boiling Springs at 8:30 a.m. I seem to go out heavier each time I go to town. The last few days have been cooler. It would be nice if it lasts, but I'm sure it will be getting hot again real soon.

I am finding lots of scrumptious red raspberries so I picked a bag for supper and breakfast, but they will probably be mush by morning. The rabbits and groundhogs are very active in this area. They just scurry along the trail as if we weren't even there. I'm seeing many indigo buntings, yellow finches, and cardinals in this area.

Water is scarce on the section from Boiling Springs to Darlington Shelter so you may need to carry additional water when you leave town. Check the data book for available resources. We crossed several roads with restaurants that will allow you to fill your water bottles. The shortage of water is partially because we are crossing lots of farmland in this area. Most of what we are hiking through, or by, is cornfields and soybean fields.

We found if we walked really fast, the mosquitoes in the boggy wetlands would leave you alone. If you stop for a break, they attack you quite viciously.

Shortly before reaching the shelter, we passed the Tuscarora Trail, which is the northern terminus, of this two-hundred-sixty-mile trail. The trail again intersects the AT in the Shenandoah National Park in Virginia.

We stopped at the Darlington Shelter after a 14.3-mile day.

Sunday-We had some good rain last night and we had to pack everything up wet, so when I got to the Doyle Hotel in Duncannon, Pennsylvania, I hung everything out the window to dry. I'm sure the neighbors love seeing it all flapping in the wind.

My throat is hurting today. I hope I'm not getting sick.

Grayson found several ticks on her today. We are hiking through a lot of farmland with high grasses so I guess this is a bad area for them. This section is very boggy and a great breeding home for mosquitoes. The weather is better today, but the humidity makes for a long, tiring hike. The climb up Hawk Mountain was gradual but worth the climb up. The views of the Susquehanna River and the town of Duncannon were spectacular. The hike down the mountain was a short one, but you have some loose rockslides to contend with.

It was an easy hike into town so we decided to stay at the historic Doyle Hotel.

The hotel is an old brick, somewhat rundown, building. Anheuser Busch originally bought the building and the Doyle family ran it for more than four decades.

They are very hiker-friendly and offer some of the best food I've had in a while. After getting settled, we went to town to take care of all our chores. Then we went down to the bar to have a few cold ones with the other hikers. Tweety's niece is picking her up for a few days, and she will catch up with us down the trail at the second shelter.

We hiked 11.4 miles today.

Monday-I had a great night's sleep at the hotel and slept until 8:00 a.m. That was a treat to be able to sleep in. Grayson is not a morning person just like LaTripper. We had the best blueberry pancakes and coffee at Jodie's Café. Duncannon has a bad rap amongst the hikers, but I found it to be a hiker-friendly town. They tried to accommodate us, but then our needs are small compared to most.

I talked to Ed last night. He has a friend who backpacks and is going to e-mail me. My list of new friends who share my love of the outdoors is growing. I met Grease Pot last night. She is from Colorado. It would be fun to look her up when Ed and I are out there sometime and do some hiking with her.

I am so glad I decided to continue my hike. I know I would have regretted getting halfway and quitting.

We left town and walked over the Clark Ferry Bridge, which spans the Susquehanna River. This bridge was named for Daniel Clark, who operated a ferry service here in 1785. This river is 444 miles long and is said to be one of the widest and longest rivers crossed on the AT.

I'm finding a lot of blackberries, but they aren't very sweet yet. The poison ivy is the worst I have ever seen. The underbrush is so dense that you can't avoid the poison hitting your legs as you go along. I need to start wearing long pants when I am in this type of terrain.

I encountered two black snakes in the trail. One was determined to stay put and kept striking at the sticks we would throw at him. Finally, Grayson took her hiking stick and lifted him out of the trail. The next one was more cooperative: after a few hits with her poles, he moved along.

Lots of rocks today, but I've been told that they are not as bad as the rumored Pennsylvania rocks ahead.

We have had fabulous views of the valley and the river all day. Water is getting harder to find again. The spring at Peters Mountain Shelter was dried up. I carried four liters out from Clarks Ferry Shelter since we were notified that there was a shortage of water ahead.

We have made it to the official halfway markers for the trail. We decided to set up camp in the woods tonight. We got in to camp early and enjoyed a relaxing evening, catching up with Tweety. We only hiked 10.9 miles today.

I found the following ditty in the register at the Eckville Hikers Center when we stopped for lunch.

An Ode to Pennsylvania

Big rocks, small rocks,
Stumble and fall rocks
Drive-me-up-the-wall rocks
Lots and lots of rocks
Gray rocks, brown rocks, and
Making me fall down rocks
Pointy, sharp, or round rocks
Rocks and rocks and rocks
Loose or in-the-ground rocks
Climbing up and down rocks
Ankle jarring, shinbone scarring
Boy it's rough
Had enough
I'm really sick of rocks
Rocks are driving me insane
Rocks are leaving me in pain
Just tell me when I'm near the end
*Of all these *#!@ rocks!!*

Author unknown

I saw another indigo bunting and a yellow goldfinch. I'm not seeing much wildlife since we got into Pennsylvania except for snakes, squirrels, and a few birds.

My new trail name is The Jolly Green Giant. They tease me because I can step over logs and rocks so easily compared to most hikers, and I usually wear green pants and shirt. It's quite amazing how handy these long legs can be.

We've passed several slack-packers going north to south today.

The weather forecast is for the nineties all week with high humidity and showers. The shelters seem to be getting farther apart so tomorrow we plan to hike 17.5 miles.

We stopped at the Peterson Mountain Shelter and hiked 11.3 miles.

Tuesday-The old Earl Shaffer Shelter is still standing at Peters Mountain. I'm glad they don't all look like that now. It was a very long day today. We only had one climb, but the rest of the trail was very rocky with trees across the trail every six feet or so. We had to climb over, under, or around them. The breeze kept the heat tolerable. We did not have any views today just trudging along the rocks. I miss all the beautiful spring flowers we saw in the south.

I put my music on today and seemed to be flying down the trail. I don't know where my newfound energy came from. About three in the afternoon, the bottom fell out, and I was ready to be done. I would love to have a few more days like that. I heard Tweety say to Grayson, "I guess the Ever-Ready Bunny finally ran out." I heard from another hiker that Jagged sprained her ankle today for the second time.

We decided to pitch our tents by the river instead of going to the shelter.

Our total miles today were 18.3.

Wednesday-It has been a long hot day with rocks, rocks, and more rocks, and this is just the beginning of Pennsylvania. There weren't any views today, but if there were, I would have missed them because I had to watch my every step so my eyes were always on my feet. I wouldn't mind the rocks so much, but every other rock is loose, just waiting to trip you up.

The only wildlife I am seeing today is squirrels, chipmunks, and a few birds. I did see a hummingbird moth, which looks like a hummingbird but is only one inch long. It hovers just like the bird. The bugs are really bad again today. If you keep moving, they pretty much leave you alone, but who can hike for twenty-four hours a day?

The shelter has well water, a solar shower, and tent sites. The caretaker lives next door, and he sells ice cream and sodas for a reasonable price. I slept in the bunkhouse, but the only bunk left was an upper one. I didn't get much air so it was very hot, along with the other hikers who wanted to party all night long. We stopped at the 501 Shelter after 15.7 miles.

Thursday-The Eagles Nest Shelter has a compost privy. I think this is a fairly new system that seems to be working as long as you do your part and put some of the compost material in each time you go potty. We heard that Yeich Springs near the shelter and every spring north had dried up and that we should get water at Sand Spring and carry it into camp.

I passed the trail to the historic Pilger Ruh Spring and then began my ascent to the vista at Round Head. Look for the trail on the right to Shower Steps that will lead down to PA 501 and a spring. From there, I passed Hartlein Campsite and spring, which was also dried up, and then began a gradual climb out of the valley to the Ridge of Blue Mountain. Just past the crossing of PA 183, I came to the Fort Dietrich Snyder Marker. It marks the spot where, in 1705, there was a lookout post to warn of approaching enemies during the French and Indian Wars. We are at 1,440 feet elevation at this marker.

From here, I passed the Sand Spring Trail. This is our last water source before we reach the shelter, two miles north of here. The water was no longer running. All that was left was a pool that was about to dry up. The water was not very desirable, but at least it was water. We hauled enough water up to the shelter to get through dinner and breakfast, and north up the trail until we reach Port Clinton, which is 9.3 miles farther north.

The extra water we are carrying is really adding weight we don't need with all this heat and humidity. We could take advantage of all the road crossings, but we are too tired to hike the extra miles into town.

The terrain was better today, but it was hotter than yesterday. I felt dizzy all day and found out later that Grayson was having the same problems. I think it's a combination of the heat, not drinking enough water, and having to look down at each step, all day long.

We have bats in the shelter tonight, but since bats eat bugs, we will have one less annoyance to keep us up all night.

We stayed at Eagles Nest Shelter after hiking fifteen miles.

Friday-We followed the rolling and rocky ridge of Blue Mountain for another six miles through woodlands, open meadows, and a few more road crossings before we began our nine-hundred-foot descent into Port Clinton. It's steep at the bottom, but the thought of a day in town keeps my feet flying.

I saw a four-foot rattlesnake as I was leaving camp this morning. As usual, it was so very hot again. My energy was so low, and I was getting disappointed at the lack of water along the trail. We did find water in a pond filled with frogs and smelled nasty, but once we filtered the water, it tasted okay.

We finally made it to Port Clinton after crossing the Schuylkill River. We decided to stay at the Port Clinton Hotel since the B&B wanted $139. The hotel had just put in air-conditioning in all the rooms or I would have stayed in the pavilion and saved some money. I needed the AC to cool off. The pavilion has an outhouse and is free to the hikers. It was almost full with hikers. Tonight, after we got settled in, we decided to check out the town. We found the Peanut House and bought some dried fruit, candy, and nuts.

We had a great lunch at the hotel and decided to take a rest before heading out again. At 9:00 p.m., we went down and had some nachos and all the fixings, with two beers to wash it all down. We went to the outfitters, and while we were there, they told us about Fred, who would shuttle us around at no cost. We looked him up, and he took us into Hamburg for food. We offered him gas money, but he would not take it. They said he looks forward to this time of year and meeting all the hikers.

We only hiked 8.6 miles today.

Saturday-I had a wonderful rest and an excellent breakfast at Three C's Restaurant. We spoke with some hikers at breakfast that had two rattlesnake encounters. One hiker decided to kill one and cook it for lunch today and have the skin stretched out on a piece of wood. On the way out of the restaurant, a local informed us that it is illegal to kill rattlers in Pennsylvania and that they are protected here.

I spoke with Ed last night. He was working and sounded as lonely as I am for his company. I do miss him so much.

We were back on the trail at noon, and we were informed that there was no water at the shelter where we plan on stopping, but there is a spring three miles south of the shelter. I am carrying food for four days. I am eating so much now. Four days feel like seven.

I have now completed 1,203.3 miles and have 955.7 miles to go.

I saw a hummingbird while I was sitting at camp tonight. I think my red hat was attracting him. All the birds seem to be very active tonight. Today is my youngest son's birthday. He is now thirty-three years old but still my baby.

Hiking was much easier today. We hiked until five in the afternoon. There is not much to write about in this section of Pennsylvania except rocks, rocks, heat, and bugs. We just seem to be putting one foot in front of the other, day after day.

The Windsor Furnace Shelter is small but cozy. The birds are singing, and the fireflies are lighting up the bushes as we sit and relax for the night. It appears someone just turned on the Christmas lights as they begin to flicker on and off.

There was an entry in the register by Renegade, quoting a song by Travis Tritt. The song is "It's a Great Day to Be Alive." How true!

I am totally a part of nature out here. I am one with nature. Every time we go to town, I meet someone who sincerely cares about our needs. They offer to take you to the grocery store, bank, ATM, etc. and won't take any money for their time. I hope when Ed and I decide to settle down, it will be in a small town where people still care about others. I guess that's why I left Florida. I don't think I could go back to that fast-paced life again. My head would be spinning after being out here.

This area is known for Windsor Furnace, and the ironworks cast from them. It dates back to the 1800s.

We only hiked 6.1 miles today.

Sunday-Every day is planned around water availability. So far we are managing to find sources. You have to really plan ahead and carry out extra.

Grayson bought a pair of new sandals. They are called Bites, and they have teeth on the bottoms. She said they would eat up the trail. We have renamed her Trex since they are so big and bulky.

The three of us are having a great time out here. Some days, we talk all day, and others, we walk quietly with our own thoughts and enjoy just being out here. I guess I can I say I am truly blessed.

The climb up to Pulpit Rock was steady, all uphill, but it was a fairly good terrain. We climbed 897 feet in four and a half miles. I was so disappointed to finally get to the top to find it fogged in. I was told that these were some of the best views in Pennsylvania. There are views of Palmerton as you hike along the Blue Ridge and views of Allentown and South Mountain to the south. We decided to take a break and enjoy the cooler breeze up here. It looks like we could get some rain today. It's funny that there are no birds singing up here. I don't know if it is the elevation or what. We continued climbing another two hundred feet to the Pinnacle.

We found a huge rock pile where every hiker adds a rock. It stands about fifteen feet high. We did our part and added one rock each.

We hiked two-tenths of a mile on Mountain Hawk Road to the Eckville Hikers Center, an enclosed bunkroom with space for six hikers. We filled up our bottles with water and had a cold soda and ice cream. Decided this was a good spot for a break and lunch.

Amanda, whose trail name is Love, told us she is leaving the trail today and going back to school. I will miss her since she and Kristen were my motivators when my sister left the trail. Their group is slack-packing today.

It was a long hard climb out of Eckville Hikers Center. We started from 535 feet and climbed to 1,500 feet straight up to the Kittatinny Ridge. The rocks have gone from bad to horrible. I hear the rocks only get worse going out of Lehigh Gap.

We stopped for the night at Allentown Hiking Club Shelter. It's a nice shelter, but the water is way downhill. We hiked a total of 16.5 miles today.

The following data was taken from the Appalachian Trail Thru-Hikers' Companion, 2007 edition.

> The Kittatinny Ridge, also known as Blue Mountain, is a long ridge that winds one hundred and eighty-five miles through eastern and central Pennsylvania. This section has been designated by Audubon Pennsylvania as the largest of the state's important bird areas to watch migrating hawks, eagles, and vultures. Sixteen species of hawk, falcons, and eagles have been spotted over the mountain, and each autumn, more than 20,000 raptors use the mountain's strong updrafts to help carry them south for the winter.

The best times to view the birds are in September and October.

A two-and-a-half-mile hike up the blue-blazed Trail will take you to the visitor's center. This is another spot I would like to come back and visit in the fall.[7]

Monday-We had a beautiful moon with clear skies and a gentle breeze last night. I saw a deer when I left camp this morning, near our food bags. He took off in a hurry when he saw me.

We met a nice day hiker by the name of Jim, who shared his food with us. He offered us grapes, bananas, salami, and cheese.

We hiked up PA 309 to Blue Mountain Bed and Breakfast, only to find the restaurant closed on Mondays. At least they had water for us. I was really looking forward to having pancakes. I will just have some more trail mix and a Snickers bar.

Today, we had the most challenging scramble over a vast rock field. The trail took us to the top of Bake Oven Knob over house-size boulders. I got on top of one boulder and was straddling another and wasn't sure where to go from there. Sometimes, I had to put my poles aside and just use my hands or sit down and slide down to the next rock. This section along the ridge is called Knife Rocks, Bare Rocks, and Bake Oven Rocks and is very challenging.

There wasn't any water at the Bake Oven Knob Shelter. A Trail Angel left gallon bottles of water at the shelter for us. We decided to go into Lehigh Gap tonight and head up the other side first thing tomorrow morning. We made our way to Jail House Hostel, which is an old prison. It's in the basement of the Palmerton Borough Hall, and they allow you to sleep free and use the shower. Girl Scout Troop 112 put together goodie bags for the hikers. We hiked a grueling 17.4 miles today.

Tuesday-We had a great night at the hostel and were able to get back on the trail early.

The hike out of Lehigh Gap was worse than I imagined. When I got to the top, I had one last climb up and over the boulders to get to the top, and I realized there was no climbing this one with a pack on.

---

[7] Appalachian Trail Thru-Hikers' Companion, 2007

Hot Rod offered to take my pack up since he knew I was nervous, and he came back down, put my pack on, and climbed back up. Going up the mountain meant you had to find toe and finger holds and pull yourself up and over. I was scared climbing up and was shaking by the time I got to the top. Once I made it to the top and settled down, I was able to celebrate my success and enjoy the wonderful views of Palmerton.

Since 1898, two smelters flanking the town of Palmerton have produced zinc for machinery, pharmaceuticals, and other products. As a result, thirty-three million tons of residues were dumped. The smelting resulted in large quantities of zinc, lead, cadmium, and sulfur dioxide. The emissions caused defoliation of more than 2,000 acres of all vegetation, thus causing a biological desert. After the death of the forest, severe soil erosion caused an estimated twelve to twenty-four inches of soil to be washed away from the site. The furnaces were shut down in 1980 and in 1982 the US Environmental Protection Agency placed the Palmerton site on the National Priorities List (Superfund) for remediation. The mountain is finally restoring itself. There are some detours here. Make sure you check the data books.

Water is still a major problem. We had seventeen miles between shelters and we could not find any water in between. It was about ninety-five degrees today, and all I carried out was two liters of water since I wanted to keep my weight down for the climb. We were totally exposed to the elements for about four hours today, with no trees. I went through the first liter quite fast. Luckily, someone brought eight gallons of water to the trail crossing at Little Gap and Blue Mountain Road. It's only one and a half miles to Danielsville, and we were considering hitching a ride to town for water.

After lunch, a storm started moving in. We realized we would not make it to our destination before it hit so we ran for cover. We sat under some small trees with our rain jackets and pack covers until it was over.

After going west on Smith Gap Road for one mile, we stopped for the night at Linda Gellock and John Stempa's house. They are also AT hikers and can appreciate our hardships. Their trail names were Crayola Lady and The Mechanical Man. They opened their home to any hikers who needed a place of rest and offered a hot shower and a place to sleep and cooked us a wonderful dinner of Philly steak sandwiches, salad, and iced tea. They allowed us to get on the computer to check our e-mail. The next morning, they drove us back to the trail.

I can't believe the challenges we have been presented with this past week. This week has been the most challenging for me since I began my hike. I think it's the combination of heat, lack of water, rocks, bugs, low energy, and some very difficult climbs for me.

We hiked 12.2 miles today.

Wednesday -It was a cool and misty morning. I had a great night's sleep. The girls were freezing, but Trapper Lee loved it. The temperature at the power lines was sixty-five degrees at 9:30 a.m.

I met Elmer Nelson on the trail today heading south. We got to talking and realized he was from Union Bridge, where my sister Nachette lives. He lives one road over from my sister. He also knew Loralynne, another sister, from the singles club in Westminster, Maryland. Many years ago, my brother Rodger worked for him as well.

We went into Wind Gap on PA 33, and we were planning on having lunch at the hotel only to find out there wasn't any. We just had a soda and continued up the trail since tomorrow is going to be a town day.

Most of my friends know how much I love to dance so you will appreciate this. We have created several songs and dances as we prance across the rocks. The first one is called "The Hikers Rock." When you balance on rocks for hours with nothing to step on, in between each rock, you start to rock side to side one rock to another for balance. If you put that to music, you begin to move very gracefully. The second dance we created is "The High Stepper." Just imagine your driveway full of every size and shape of rock with no flat spaces to step on. You then start high-stepping to avoid a trip and fall. When you watch your feet nonstop for twelve hours a day, you start to actually get dizzy. I guess that would be another song: "I'm So Dizzy." We have decided to make "Dizzy" our theme song for Pennsylvania. I guess that's enough foolishness for now.

Being out here taught me to appreciate the small things in life that our busy lives cause us to miss out on. I'm talking about feelings, caring, giving, sharing, or just being myself. If I choose to be silly or just downright crazy, I can. No one will judge me; they just accept me for who I am. I have overcome so many fears, mainly that of being alone. Even though I prefer not to be alone, it's okay if I am.

We had water at Kirk Ridge Shelter tonight for a change. We completed 17.3 miles.

Thursday-We had an easy hike into town and found a fabulous bakery. Reverend Karen of the Presbyterian Church of the Mountain Hostel allows long-distance hikers to stay for a minimum of two nights for three dollars. They serve you an incredible sit-down dinner. The congregation of the church supplies all the food. After dinner, a small group of us rode into town for ice cream.

Sandy, a sports medicine physical therapist, assessed my finger. It was still very red and sore. I couldn't bring the tip of my finger up. She splinted it for two weeks and said I probably damaged the ligaments. She also recommended some exercises that might help.

I have lost twenty-five pounds, and I am looking at consuming more calories instead of balancing my fat, carbohydrates, and protein. If I continue to lose weight, I'll have to drop off. I've always said I would never sacrifice my health or my safety to be out here.

Delaware Water Gap is a great little town. It's such a relaxed, slow-paced town with citizens who really care about the hikers and their needs. Some of the hikers can only see the end and their climb up Katahdin. I hope I never lose sight of why I am out here.

We stopped for the night in Delaware Water Gap after hiking only 6.4 miles.

NEW YORK AND NEW JERSEY

July 23-30, 2002

The section of trail through New York is eighty-eight miles while New Jersey is a short seventy-four miles. There is no hitchhiking allowed in New Jersey.

On the way out of town on Friday, we crossed over I-80 before we began our first climb. I am so excited to have seen my first bald eagle today while I was coming over the Delaware River Bridge.

We are now entering Worthington State Forest and climbed 1,382 feet to Sunfish Pond. The pond is a crystal clear glacial lake and reminds me so much of the ponds in Maine. We took a break by the pond so we could enjoy the serene setting. It is cool, with a nice breeze, and I had to put my jacket on for the first time in a while. It's only sixty-five degrees at noon. I saw lots of beaver activity but no beavers. I did see several wild turkeys and some deer.

One of the first twenty-three hikers to complete the entire trail was Herbert Hiller. They have placed a memorial to him along the trail in this section.

From the Delaware Water Gap, the trail follows the Kittatinny Ridge for several miles. We stayed on the ridge, with very few climbs, but the terrain was still very rocky. The view was worth the rocky trail and awarded us with some fabulous views of the valley below. From one of the ridges, where we took another break, we could see the Yards Creek Reservoir.

If you go west on Blue Mountain Lakes Road for eight-tenths of a mile, you will come to the YMCA's Camp Ken-Etiwa-Pec, a former Boy Scout camp. If you are not stopping here for the night, you can find a hand pump for water at the crossroads. The facility is located on Long Pine Pond, and they offer a screened cabin at the pond for hikers at no cost. They invited us to the dining hall for leftover salad, bread and butter, ziti, and chili. They would not take any money. As I have said before, there are real angels living among us out here. This had to be one of the most peaceful places we have found in a long time. We are the only three at camp tonight.

I love the YMCA camp and the cabin we have for the night on the water. We hiked 10.5 miles today.

Saturday-I woke this morning to the view of the pond out of the screen door, and I saw a deer on the other side of the pond. Laura, one of the employees, gave us a ride back to the trail. She is sixty-five years old and has a dream to hike the AT. We gave her some much-needed encouragement, and I hope she chooses to follow her dreams.

We passed the trail to Buttermilk Falls. I would like to come back and do the two-mile loop trail someday. Since we are experiencing a drought, the falls are probably not running very well. I was told that on a good day, there are three falls running full force.

The view of Culver's Lake was marvelous. We found lots of blueberries today. We stopped at Worthington's Bakery since we had heard they have great goodies, but we were disappointed to find that there were no pies, fruit, or coffee. The deli section was also very limited.

Grayson saw another bear today, with a collar on, and said it was climbing up a cliff but not very timid.

The terrain was much better today. We saw gliders taking off from the ridges and landing in the valley below. We sat and watched for quite some time.

There is a large group of teenagers at the shelter tonight. They are on a ten-day hike with several counselors. They are from New York, and most of them have never been exposed to living in the woods for so many days. They showed such an interest in our long-distance hike and were full of so many questions. This is a very unusual shelter.

There is a bear box for our food, but it was full by the time we put our food inside. The large group had no room for all their food, and the counselors decided to leave it in their tent. The privy is an open box, no seat, and no walls. It just sits on the ground with no trees around it. I went in search of a tree but had to go a good distance to be out of sight of the campers.

It was a very interesting night. We had just settled down in the shelter, with the larger group sitting around their campfire. All of a sudden, we heard a bear banging on the food box, trying to get inside. We chased him off and settled down for the night. Shortly after, I heard someone banging pots and pans together to scare him off again. During the night, he came back and stole one of the camper's backpacks. We found it the next morning down the hill, all torn up and with everything scattered about. About 6:00 a.m., we were awakened to the counselors yelling and chasing the bear out of camp again. He had come back into camp and tore a hole in the tent with all the food and took off with the bag. We found it spread out all over the ground. We reported the activities to a ranger the next day as we were leaving camp, and he told us that he had other reports of bear sightings, probably the same one. It's a shame that the negligence of others will more than likely cause the bear to be put down.

We had a long day today and completed twenty-one miles. We stopped at the Gren Anderson Shelter.

Sunday-The shelter was busy last night with twenty-seven campers.

I saw several bright orange salamanders today. It was misty and extremely humid today. I heard a pileated woodpecker, but I never did see him. I saw the most beautiful purple and yellow flowers today. I've missed the flowers in the past few weeks.

The terrain was getting better as we continued across the ridge, and we seem to be getting out of the worst of the rocks. The humidity in the air made all the rocks extremely slippery.

We had bottles of water waiting for us by the road crossing this morning. We also received trail magic from Greg Egan, a thru-hiker in 1993. He had a real picnic for us of hotdogs, fruit, salad, soda, chips, pasta, and more. I had eaten lunch about an hour before, but it did not stop me from eating again.

We decided to take a short detour to climb the monument in High Point State Park. The tower was built in 1930 in honor of our fallen war heroes. It stands on the highest point in New Jersey at 1,930 feet. It was still very hazy so our views were limited. I heard that you have a view of three states from the 220-foot tower.

We took the short side trail to the Jim Murray Property. The property is on eighty-four acres with a cabin, washer, dryer, well water, and limited bunks. I set up my tent under a huge maple tree in hopes of catching a nice breeze.

It was an interesting night. Amazing Grace was sleeping out on the ground under her rain fly when all of a sudden, she started screaming. A bug had crawled into her ear and was biting her. Someone had a cell phone and was able to call for help. She was escorted to a medical facility and later returned okay.

Just as things were settling down, the two donkeys out in the pasture decided it was a good time to mate. The donkeys began chasing each other around the pasture, making an awful racket as they bellowed. This went on several times throughout the night. Once I got to sleep, I had a good night's sleep.

The caretaker said it's supposed to be hotter today than yesterday. I am having thoughts of getting off the trail. I just can't handle the heat. I know everyone is hot, but it actually makes me feel ill. I also feel like I'm wearing down physically. I've lost so much weight now.

We had another long day and hiked 20.3 miles.

Monday-We only hiked 1.8 miles today. I woke up to a tree full of birds greeting me with their songs. It never cooled off last night. I woke to the heat and humidity, and by the time we hiked into Unionville, my boots were wet with the sweat dripping off my face.

I made the important decision to drop off the trail today. Tweety was so upset to see me leave. She hugged and hugged me with big tears rolling down her cheeks. She said she understood why I had to leave, but she would miss me terribly. Amazing Grace said she would watch out for her. A few more hugs, and I was on my way home.

I called my brother, who lived nearby, to pick me up, and I spent the night with him. The next day, I caught a bus to Frederick, Maryland where I spent several days eating and getting some much-needed rest. I will drive to Maine to be with my Eddie in a few days.

It has been an experience one would only dream of having. I am very pleased with my accomplishments, and I feel okay about discontinuing my hike.

If someone were to ask me why I decided to hike the trail or what I got out of it, I would have to say the wonderful new friends I have made along the trail and the caring townspeople who don't think twice about helping you in any way possible. It might be a hot shower, or a computer to write home, and sometimes a bed to sleep in. They were always willing to shuttle you to town or wherever you needed to go. I can't list them all as I would surely miss someone.

Also the new friends I have made, who are also attempting a thru-hike, section hike, day hike, or just out for the weekend. The encouragement they gave me kept me going on my bad days, lifted my spirits on a low day, and became my family when I was homesick. I will hold each of you close to my heart forever. Please stay in touch with me, and let me know how your hike is going.

I am now a section-hiker and will attempt to finish the Appalachian Trail as my new life and time will allow.

Life is all about adventures…..

CONNECTICUT

In 2008, I hiked a small portion of the trail in Connecticut. Fifty-two miles of the Appalachian Trail passes through Connecticut. You can expect elevations from 260 to 2,316 feet. The best time to hike this section is May through early October.

HIGHEST POINTS IN CONNECTICUT

The highest point is the south slope of Mount Frissell, Salisbury at the Massachusetts and Connecticut line at 2,380 feet.

- Bear Mountain, Salisbury at 2,320 feet
- Round Mountain, Salisbury at 2,296 feet
- Gridley Mountain, Salisbury at 2,210 feet
- Bald Peak, Salisbury at 2,110 feet
- Bradford Mountain, Canaan at 1,962 feet
- Bald Mountain, Norfolk at 1,770 feet
- Crissey Ridge, Norfolk at 1,770 feet
- Twinpeaks, Canaan Mountain, Canaan at 1,740 feet
- Lions Head, Salisbury at 1,738 feet
- Stone Man Mountain, Canaan at 1,732 feet

Connecticut has eighteen designated camping areas, seven with shelters. Camping is permitted in only those areas because of the narrowness of the trail corridor and its proximity to private land and because of the large number of people using the trail.

The Housatonic River Valley to the east and the Taconic Range to the west are particularly scenic.

Many sections run along the banks of rivers. Hiking is mostly moderate, with steep, fairly challenging sections that are short in duration. Views are often pastoral. The trail passes through the northern hardwood forest—a large, rather homogeneous plant community interspersed with meadows, wetlands, streams, cultivated land, and settled areas.

Most mammals are nocturnal or more active at dawn or dusk. Common, yet not likely to be seen, are the flying squirrels. Familiar daytime mammals you may see are the red squirrel, gray squirrel, chipmunks, and the woodchuck or groundhog. You may also encounter cottontail rabbits, raccoons, gray fox, and red fox.

Shrews are among the world's smallest mammals and require almost constant nourishment. If you see tunnels across the trail, it is probably from the moles.[8]

MASSACHUSETTS

The trail in Massachusetts passes through ninety miles of New England. The elevation changes are from 650 to 3,491 feet. The best time to hike this section is May through early October. The state bird is the black-capped chickadee.

The Appalachian Trail here leads through the Berkshires. Pleasant stretches through wooded hills and valleys feature such outstanding peaks as Mt. Greylock and Mount Everett, and the trail passes through several small towns. Drinking water is not a problem in this area. Several summits and ledges provide views, and there are long, flat sections atop the Berkshire Plateau quite different from the dry ridge walks of the mid-Atlantic and Virginias. Ascents, though sometimes steep, are seldom sustained.[9]

---

[8] Information provided by the Appalachian Trail Guide to Massachusetts and Connecticut, 11th edition, and the Appalachian Trail Conference, Harpers Ferry, © by Ken Wadness.

[9] Massachusetts information provided by the Appalachian Trail Guide to Massachusetts and Connecticut, Eleventh Edition, and the Appalachian Trail Conference, Harpers Ferry, © 2000 by Ken Wadness.

Bascom Lodge and Saddle Ball Mountain from Mount Greylock

VERMONT

The Trail enters Vermont after crossing the Connecticut River. After joining up with the Long Trail at Sherburne Pass, the two trails are contiguous for 95 miles through the Green Mountains.

This section of the trail is 145 miles long with elevation changes of 400 to 4,010 feet. The lushness of this state makes it one of the most beautiful of all the sates along the trail. The AT passes through high, rugged country with woods and overgrown farmlands. The AT approaches tree line at the Killington and Stratton mountains, and parts feature strenuous ascents. But in general, Vermont hiking crosses varied terrain, at lower- to mid-range elevations with a fair amount of elevation gain and loss. It passes through forests of paper birch and white pine, wooded mountains, and farm valleys.

The Green Mountain National Forest follows the backbone of Vermont north from the Massachusetts border for one hundred miles all the way to Appalachian Gap. Within its boundaries are cold streams and beaver ponds famous for brook and rainbow trout fishing. Some overnight sites charge a fee.

Avoid Vermont Trails from mid-April through Memorial Day. They can be very muddy, and sloppy conditions lead to serious trail erosion.

In the Northeast, Green Mountain state is revered as a rough-cut refuge from city life. You will hike through sugar maple, white birch, and conifer forests on the same paths that Native Americans and French Canadian fur trappers traversed. You will be walking on the rocks and roots of 19th-century carriage paths gone to seed. The Green Mountain National Forest follows the backbone of Vermont north from the Massachusetts border for over one hundred miles and goes all the way to Appalachian Gap. Within its boundaries are cold streams and beaver ponds famous for brook and rainbow-trout fishing.

The upper gorge of the Mill River is crossed at its head by a suspension bridge over which carries the Long Trail. There are some cascades immediately below the bridge and more rapids and short drops at various spots throughout the gorge. Downstream, the gorge gets deeper and deeper, approaching 90' in depth at its deepest.

I hope to hike Vermont in 2013.

Vermont is worth seeing, over and over. It's not just the colors in the fall it's the snap in the air, the V-formations of Canada geese overhead, the racket of the wind rattling countless dry leaves, perfect beaver ponds, mountain views, and boulder strewn streams in the forest and along the Appalachian Trail.

Clarendon Gorge and the Mill River

NEW HAMPSHIRE

In New Hampshire, the trail reaches the most exposed and difficult terrain along the AT. The trail enters New Hampshire when you cross the Ledyard Bridge in Hanover. There are elevation changes of 400 to 6,288 feet. Consider hiking the section that passes through the White Mountains in July or August and the remaining miles from June to September.

The state flower is the lilac, and there are 161 miles in this section.

White Mountain National Forest, better known as the Whites, is one of America's most popular public lands, registering more visitors annually than Yellowstone and Yosemite combined.

The Forest Service works closely with the Appalachian Mountain Club and has made great strides toward minimizing the impact of crowds on the Whites while keeping them open to all who want to sample the grandeur of the Northeast's highest peaks, the Presidential Range.

The hut system is a series of beautiful mountain lodges that provide food, shelter, and creature comforts for hikers. They are all about one day of hiking apart, which allows you to carry less. You need to make reservations to stay in the huts, which don't come cheap, and even lean-tos and tent platforms come with a fee. 5 The White Mountains are a mountain range that covers about a quarter of the state and a small portion of western Maine. Most of the area is public land, including the White Mountain National Forest, as well as a number of state parks. Its most famous peak is Mount Washington, which at 6,288 feet is the highest mountain in the Northeastern US and home to the fastest surface wind gusts recorded at 231 miles per hour measured in the Northern Hemisphere. Mount Washington is part of the Presidential Range. The Whites include several smaller groups including the Franconia Range, Sandwich Range, Carter-Moriah Range, Kinsman Range, and Pilot Range.[10]

---

[10] The above information was taken from Appalachian Trail Guide, New Hampshire & Vermont, 10th Edition, 2001, and Appalachian Trail Conservancy, Harpers Ferry, WV.

I have not had the opportunity to hike any of the Appalachian Trail through New Hampshire.

Franconia Ridges

Kim "Sketcher" Sevy on Mt Lafayette

MAINE

Maine's state flower is the white pine cone and tassel.

Most of the trail in Maine is not recommended for novice hikers. Maine's 281 miles are generally considered the most difficult of all fourteen states. Some parts require grabbing onto tree roots and limbs to climb or descend and are especially slippery and hazardous in wet weather.

Lakes, streams, and bogs abound. While that makes a moose or a loon common sights, it also makes for a muddy tread way and many fords of mountain streams. Some of these fords, notably the Kennebec River, can be difficult and potentially life-threatening when water is high. Wait until the waters subside or backtrack and find a road to follow, if one exists. You are more than likely to see a moose feeding in one of the many lakes throughout Maine.

The Appalachian Trail in Maine has elevations that range from 490 to 5,267 feet. There is a chain of forty lean-tos and campsites providing accommodations along the trail.[11]

The 281 miles in Maine can be roughly divided into three segments: The eastern section is sometimes called the One-Hundred Mile Wilderness, which runs between Katahdin and Monson. This section comprises disconnected mountains, lakes, ponds, streams, and forest. While this section has a flatter profile than other parts of Maine, it has special challenges. The mountains are relatively low but present some very rugged climbs. Stream crossings here can be tricky in high water. Re-supply is scarce in this isolated but heavily used area.

---

[11] The above information was taken from Appalachian Trail Guide to Maine, Thirteenth Edition, published by the Maine Appalachian Trail Club, Inc., 1996

The central section, between Monson and the Bigelow Preserve, features a short, rugged stretch followed by some of the least strenuous hiking in Maine and a crossing of the widest un-bridged river along the trail, the Kennebec. A free canoe service will ferry hikers across the river. Fording this river is extremely dangerous because the water level can rise rapidly and without warning.

The western section is an area of extremely steep, four-thousand-foot Mountains, arguably the toughest part of the entire trail.

It includes the notorious mile-long boulder scramble of Mahoosuc Notch. The boulders on the section of trail present obstacles that must be climbed over and sometimes under, creating a unique hiking experience. There are occasional ten-foot drops and places where packs must be removed to squeeze beneath a boulder. Many hikers call this stretch one of the slowest on the entire trail. It has gained the reputation of being tagged the Toughest Mile or the Killer Mile.

Monson is a town in Piscataquis County, Maine with a population of 686. The town is located on Route 15 which is a major route north to the well-known Moosehead Lake Region, to which Monson is sometimes considered a gateway. This route ultimately leads to the Canadian Province of Quebec. It is the last town located on the Appalachian Trail at the entrance to the one-hundred wilderness. Several lodging places in town cater directly to hikers.

Section-Hiker—Life Afterwards

August 2002-August 2009

After a few days of rest at my sister's house, I drove to Maine, and what a reunion I had with Ed. I don't know if I could ever leave him for that long again.

I have plunged full speed into the daily routines of life. I started my new career of painting houses, and I am staying in Camden, Maine for the summer and trying to adjust back into society.

I try to ignore the draw to be back out on the trail. It is very hard to adjust to the traffic and work and just being in crowds of people.

My Appalachian Trail adventure was so good for me. I am forever a changed person and have more confidence in myself. I seem to be a better listener, have improved my social skills, and I am more aware of the environmental impact we have placed on this beautiful land of ours. I miss being out there but not as much as I thought. I plan on section-hiking whenever possible. To be out in a setting like the Appalachian Mountains is as much a spiritual experience as it is a physical one. There is camaraderie amongst your fellow hikers unlike in the real world.

I've been struggling with spells of depression since I got off the trail. In a few days, I would be completing the trail if I had stayed on. I keep praying for peace of mind and ask that I just be happy, excited, and proud for those who will finish. I've been having problems sleeping at night for the past few weeks. I keep getting flashbacks of places and events on the trail. I don't want to lose my memories of this adventure, but I hope I can find peace with myself.

I have done some traveling with Ed since I got off the trail. We have spent a summer in Alaska and a couple of summers in the West prospecting for gold. We try to plan a sister's trip each year and have been fortunate to see Costa Rica, Jamaica, Cozumel, Grand Cayman, and Bermuda. I have made two trips to Italy and plan on continuing to travel as long as I am physically and financially able.

There is nothing like a wilderness journey for rekindling the fires of life. Simplicity is part of it—cutting the cackle. Transportation reduced to leg or arm power, eating irons to one spoon. Such simplicity, together with sweat and silence, amplify the rhythms of any long journey, especially through unknown, untattered territory. And in the end such a journey can restore an understanding of how insignificant you are—and thereby set you free.

Colin Fletcher

ABOL BRIDGE TO KATAHDIN CAMPGROUND, MAINE

October 2002

Ed and I are going to meet Grayson and Tweety in Millinocket and celebrate with them as they prepare to complete the final climb of their journey. They will be joining several other hikers for their climb up Katahdin.

My sister was going to join me in Maine, but she had a relapse from her Lyme disease. She has really been struggling with this illness. Please take precautions while hiking in the outdoors.

I coordinated our surprise with Tweety's husband and met him at the hotel. We hid in the room and jumped out to surprise her when they came into the room. We all cried and hugged, so happy to see each other. We joined all the hikers for dinner and spent hours catching up on hiker stories and all the events I missed out on.

I hiked from Abol Bridge to Katahdin Campground with Tweety and her husband, Jag and her husband, and Big Red. It was such a wonderful day to be back on the trail with good friends. I could feel the air of excitement as they neared their final destination. They invited me to climb Katahdin the next day, but I declined.

We saw some moose feeding in the pond near Katahdin Campground. The views of Double Cap and Katahdin were fabulous. We took the side trail to Big Niagara Falls for lunch and enjoyed cooling our feet in the waters.

Most of the day, we had clear skies with a light breeze and a touch of fall in the air. The trail was littered with red, yellow, and orange leaves. Fall is quickly approaching.

Katahdin from Abol Bridge, Maine

Kennebec River Crossing

UNIONVILLE TO BEAR MOUNTAIN, NEW YORK

Summer of 2004

LaTripper and I went back out on the trail at Unionville, New York, where I left off in 2002. We drove to New York and spent the night with our brother. The next morning, Frank drove us to the trail head.

We hit the trail at about 10:00 a.m. on Saturday. It felt so good to be back out on the trail again. We were just reminiscing and chattering away when we realized we had not seen any white blazes for several miles. We backtracked and found the trail, but we had gone two miles out of the way. A good thing, it was easy terrain. The mosquitoes were really bad, which surprised me since it is October. We crossed over the river, which was flooded up to the road, and followed the road for about two miles around the boggy areas. There was quite a bit of flooding in the wildlife refuge also.

We spent the night at Pochuck Mountain Shelter with Crash and Burn. They only need to complete this section north to Kent, Connecticut, and they will have completed the entire trail.

We played cards until the mosquitoes drove us inside our tents. Sis and I chose to sleep in our tents since the bugs were so bad.

We only hiked 5.3 miles since we got such a late start.

Saturday-I was nervous about crossing the river. I read an entry in the register that said two days ago, the river had been over its banks, and they had to cross in water that was up to their waists. It was down when we got there, and we crossed over without any problems.

We had an interesting day with a wide variety of terrain. We walked through the bogs on boardwalks for about two miles. The volunteers have done a great job here. Once we got through the boggy area, the bugs weren't quite as bad. We came over several stiles and through a cow pasture, with all the cows, and had to sidestep all the patties.

When we came out at New Jersey 94 on Heavon Hill Farm, they were having their October Pumpkin Festival. The people in the house next to the festival let us leave our packs on their porch and sit in the shade under a huge maple tree.

After we walked around the festival and filled our bellies with all sorts of goodies, we began the big climb up Wawayanda Mountain. After two years of being off the trail, it was a challenge, but we made it. The terrain was rocky, but we had some switchbacks to help us reach the top. We took a short detour to see the view from the top of Pinwheel Vista, which was absolutely breathtaking.

My knee did well; my feet were slightly sore. But I don't have any blisters yet.

We camped in the woods near Barrett Road next to a nice stream. We were trying to make it to Wawayanda Shelter, but we were much too tired to push on any farther.

We completed ten miles today.

Sunday-We took a slow morning out of camp today about 9:45. It was nice not having the pressure of daily deadlines, miles, or making it to town by a scheduled date. It was an easy walk to the Wawayanda Shelter, where we stopped for lunch.

We passed the trail to Wawayanda State Park Headquarters. If we hadn't stopped at the shelter, we would have stopped for water since it was only four-tenths of a mile.

It seemed we were crossing streams and swamps every couple of miles today. I'm glad we did not come out two weeks ago since there are considerable signs of flooding from all the rains. The rocks are very mossy and very pretty but just another slip hazard for us. My knee was doing okay, but my ankle was swollen and sore. We had some climbs up to the ridge and then walked for about five miles along the ridge with continuous views of Greenwood Lake. The vista at Prospect Rock offered some extraordinary views.

Sis hated the down hills and got into a situation that scared her. Twice she took her pack off and just tossed it over the side and continued to climb down. I never laughed so hard.

Our goal was to make it to Wildcat Shelter, but we decided to stop near Furnace Brook, near a small waterfall. The shelters don't seem to be spaced as well as in the southern states. I guess if you are a thru-hiker, you are kicking out more miles each day.

We completed nine miles today. I loved sleeping near the water and listening to the gurgling water all night long.

Monday-We were out of camp by nine fifteen today. We continued to cross several streams again and then we started climbing up Mount Peter, which is only 1,433 feet. The first half of our climb up the Stairway to Heaven was relatively simple. My sister did not like this section and called it "The Stairway to Hell." From there, it starts to climb more rapidly and then becomes very steep. Partway up there is a ladder you need to climb. Sis went up first without her backpack. She had me throw things up to lighten her pack and then I handed her pack up. In the process, she lost one of her water bottles. I climbed up with my pack on but did not like the climb. Once we got over the top, we had a steep descent. My sister again tossed her pack down ahead of her and continued down the steep climb.

We continued along the ridge for most of the day with views of Greenwood Lake. We almost took the side trail down to the lake but decided against it. From the ridge, we began to stroll through the woods. We thought we had it made but we came to another challenging climb. Thankfully, there was a blue-blazed trail going around. We were both too tired to make another climb.

We stopped at Wildcat Shelter after completing 7.4 miles. We are the only ones at the shelter tonight with a south-bounder tenting nearby.

Tuesday-The day started out absolutely perfect in the mid-thirties. We had a good descent down to Lakes Road then up to Fitzpatrick Falls. The falls cascade for twenty-five feet and are some of the most beautiful falls I have ever seen. I could have spent the entire day above the falls. I loved the rock scramble up the falls. We crossed the stream above the falls several times. The rocks were all covered with moss, making it so serene and peaceful.

We enjoyed the falls for a bit and continued hiking steadily up to Mombasha High Point. We did get a limited view of the New York City skyline.

The day went well until we came to a vertical rock climb up Buchanan Mountain, with no way to go around. We began to panic but decided to try going up instead of backtracking. The climb up

Buchanan Mountain was difficult for two old ladies. I got stuck and couldn't go up or down. LaTripper talked me up to the next climb. Halfway up, LaTripper slipped and grabbed onto two roots and had the ledge stuck between her legs. I was above so I removed my pack while balancing on a small ledge and managed to get her pack off and pulled it up and over with me. Then I helped pull her up and over. If we weren't so shaky, we could have had a good laugh at my sister, all covered with mud from her face down from hugging the mountain. At that point, we had to get our packs back on and continue the climb up.

Once we settled down, we chose to continue on and hoped for the best. As soon as we got to the top, the terrain was better. We came to what we thought was New York 17 and decided to hike the two miles to the hotel since it was already five thirty in the afternoon.

Well, we were only as far as Orange Turnpike with one more hour of hiking if we went back to the trail. While we were walking down Orange Turnpike, we heard a car burning rubber with their tires. As we got a little farther along, we saw police cars and officers heading into the woods, as if they were looking for someone. We had considered camping in the woods and continuing on tomorrow when this happened. Another reason we decided against setting up camp here is there was signs posted that this was a hunting area.

We spoke with someone who was filling water bottles at the spring, and he informed us that we were not at New York 17 yet. He drove us to the hotel in town and said he would wait to see if they had a vacant room before he left. They said they did not have any vacancies, but I think we just looked too wild from being in the woods for a few days. He offered to take us to Harriman, which was another five miles. We were able to find a hotel and thanked him for the ride. Shortly after settling in, we had a call from the front desk. The guy who gave us a ride found some things we had left in the truck and said he would drop them off in the morning on his way to work. Most people would not have bothered to come all the way back to the hotel.

We only hiked eight miles today.

We took Wednesday and Thursday off. We took a bus from Monroe to Middletown and called our sister-in-law to pick us up. We thought we would pick up our car and do some day hikes along the AT. We spent the day and night with our brother Frank then left on Friday in LaTripper's car after shopping for additional supplies.

We drove to Harriman State Park and hiked north to south from Arden Valley Road and Route 87 to Orange Turnpike and back for a total of five miles. We slack-packed all day and enjoyed losing some of the weight we had been carrying. We then parked at Elk Pen and walked to the Orange Turnpike and came north on the AT to complete the remaining section of the Sterling Forest.

It was a bit hotter today, but we did much better with the rock climbs. We decided to get a cabin for three nights on Lake Sebago and do some slack-packing on the trail. We went out exploring in the car after dark and saw several deer along the road. All the cabins are closing on Monday for the season so we will drive to Bear Mountain and explore the mountain and continue hiking from there.

> Harriman State Park and Bear Mountain were the first completed sections of the Appalachian Trail. Sterling Forest is located between Greenwood Lake and Arden. Six miles of the Appalachian Trail pass through the northern portion of this 20,000-acre tract.

Friday-I was up early, made my coffee, and walked down to the lake. I am beginning to relax and become one with nature again. I hate it when I get into a rush and seem to always be pushing myself to work harder. Sometimes, I am my own worst enemy.

We went to explore Greenwood Lake and hit some yard sales in the morning. We hiked a short distance on the Ramapo-Dunderberg at Tiorati Beach and followed it until it connected with the trail at the William Brien Memorial Shelter. From there, we hiked south on the trail to Arden Valley Road and back to our car. We saw several deer again today. At the shelter, they had a bonfire and a scary trail walk for Halloween. We didn't complete many AT miles, but we had so much fun exploring today.

Saturday-We hiked out by 10:00 a.m. and hiked until 4:00 p.m. It was nice and cool today with a nice touch of fall in the air.

We started at Tiorati Beach parking lot and went west on Arden Valley Road. We picked up the AT there and headed south to the Lemon Squeezer. The Lemon Squeezer is an AT landmark, which is a narrow corridor through the rock where you really have to squeeze through while pulling your pack behind you. We spent time visiting with some day hikers and enjoyed a leisurely lunch. I love the forest in this section. The leaves are beginning to change very quickly now, and I am seeing a lot of yellow, reds, and oranges. The sprawling lakes with all the fall color are simply amazing. We were able to see Upper Lake Cohasset, Island Pond and Lake Tiorati.

Lake Tiorati is a native word meaning "sky-like."

Sunday-We checked out of the cabin. It was really cold in the cabin since there were no coverings on the windows. LaTripper put her tent fly over them to block the cold wind.

We decided to take a break from hiking and went to explore Bear Mountain. We took the Perkins Memorial Scenic Drive up to Bear Mountain. We had excellent views of Bear Mountain Bridge, where the AT crosses the Hudson River. We did a short distance north on the AT to see if we could get a view from there. I felt like I could fly standing on top of Bear Mountain. I could have stayed on top absorbing the views forever if the wind hadn't been so cold. We went to the Bear Mountain Inn for the October Festival and some good German food and dancing. Sis and I tried to do the polka, but we did not do very well. We strolled along the AT through the zoo and walked down to the Bear Mountain Bridge. The bridge was built in 1924. We walked down to the bridge to see where the trail crosses the river. We found a hotel in Fort Montgomery for the night.

I took the following information from The Thru-hiker's Handbook, 2008 edition, published by Bob McCaw, but this book is no longer available.

The Trailside Museums and Wildlife Center was built in 1927. The AT goes through Trailside (but not after 5:00 p.m. when the gates are locked), passing geology, nature study, small animal, and history museums, and a well-known memorial to Walt Whitman. The exhibits feature plants and animals native to the area, and the center serves as a wildlife refuge and rehabilitation center since all animals on exhibit are disabled and unable to survive in the wild. At one hundred and twenty-four feet above sea level, the path in front of the bear exhibit is the lowest point on the entire AT.

Bear Mountain is one of the highest points on the Trail in New York at 1,305 feet. It offers views of the Hudson River Valley and the New York City skyline. There is no water on the summit.[12]

We spent most of the day on Monday yellow-blazing and checked out West Point Military Academy in Fort Montgomery. We also drove to Stoney Point Lighthouse on the Hudson and walked the historical paths. From there, we drove up to Mohunk Mountain House. I have never seen such an incredible place. The landscaping and the views of the surrounding mountains make this the perfect destination for a vacation. This is a Victorian castle, and since the rooms begin at $226 to $459 for a single room per night, I will probably never vacation here. They also have gardens that must be fabulous in the summer. After leaving the castle, we went to High Falls and walked the D&H Canal towpath.

Tuesday we spent the day at Sam's Point Preserve in Cragsmoor, New York, which is outside of Ellensville.

Sam's Point is a 4,600-acre tract with ridge-top dwarf-pine barrens. It's also part of the 90,000-acre Northern Schawangunk Mountains, whose cliffs, summits, and plateaus form a unique landscape of extraordinary ecological significance.

We started with a nice walk to the ice caves and explored the caves before turning around and hiking back. We then took the trail to Verkeerderkill Falls. It meanders through open dwarf pine, with views of the cliffs facing Gertrude's Nose and Margaret's Cliff. The ground-

---

[12] Information compiled from The Thru-hiker's Handbook, 2008 edition, published by Bob McCaw.

cover foliage was scarlet red as far as you could see. The falls were fabulous with one-hundred-foot cascades that fell so delicately down a very steep cliff. On the way back, we stopped at Sam's Point and enjoyed the views of the Schawangunk Ridge. I was told that on a clear day, you could see High Point, New York. On the way down, we ran into trail friends, Chilly Willy and Just Ray. We had great fun catching up on our days out on the trail.

I still remember the night we ended up in the same shelter as Chilly Willy and Just Ray. It had been a challenging day and we were so tired we were almost giddy. When we finally crawled into the shelter for the night our friends were already tucked in and sound asleep. We shared our day between us in a muffled voice careful not to wake the sleeping couple. All of a sudden something struck our fancy and we began to giggle. It became contagious and all three of us were laughing until we had tears coming down our cheeks. Every time we tried to muffle the noise it got worse. This continued on for almost ten minutes. The next morning we apologized only to find out they never heard us since they slept with ear plugs. Even in adversity we can find a reason to laugh.

Verkeerderkill Waterfalls—by Larry Chapman

BAXTER STATE PARK IN MAINE

Summer of 2007

I decided to do some hiking in Baxter State Park to see if I still had the endurance to someday complete the entire trail. Charlie Hugo, a very good friend of mine, and I camped outside of Baxter State Park and drove into Baxter each day to hike sections of the AT and other trails throughout the Park.

Baxter State Park is owned by the people of Maine and was a gift from Percival Baxter.

The Park contains many unusual and rare plants, animals, and landforms. Because of its extreme weather Katahdin has alpine plants, some of which are found nowhere else in Maine, and a number of rare bird and small animal species of interest and concern. Katahdin, the northern terminus of the AT, is one of its most outstanding features rising as an isolated, massive, gray granite monolith from the central Maine forest.

Katahdin is a magical name. It should stand by itself in language as it does in nature. We honor the mountain by adopting the original Abenaki Native American name for it. The translation of their name, Katahdin, is "greatest mountain." Therefore, if we interpose Mount or Mt. as part of the name, it then becomes Mount Greatest Mountain.[13]

The northern terminus of the Appalachian Trail is Baxter Peak on Katahdin, Maine's highest mountain.

There is no camping inside Baxter State Park after October 15th, and climbing Katahdin is determined on a day-by-day basis, depending on weather conditions.

---

[13] The above information was provided from the book Katahdin, A Guide to Baxter State Park and Katahdin, fifth edition, published by Clark Books, 2003 Clark Books.

There is no work-for-stay in Baxter, and regulations require every hiker entering BSP via the AT to register at the information kiosk at Abol Stream as they enter park lands, and again at Katahdin Stream with a ranger as they begin or end their hike.

The Trail up Katahdin is arguably the most difficult climb on the entire AT. Allow for a full eight to ten hours for a round trip hike of Katahdin. Following the AT up Katahdin requires rock scrambling and the use of hands in some places, and can be a frightening climb for those with even a mild fear of heights.[14]

We decided to hike the 3.3-mile Chimney Pond Trail up to the north side of Katahdin and the Great Basin. Chimney Pond is enclosed on three sides by the two-thousand-foot walls of the Great Basin. You can reach Dudley Trail, Cathedral Trail, Saddle Trail, Knife's Edge Trail, Hamlin Ridge Trail;, and Blueberry Knoll Trail from here. They have shelters to stay at so you can start out fresh the next day. When we got to the pond, we were told that the mountain had been fogged in all day, and we probably would not have a view. When we came through the trees, the mountain was in full view, but within ten minutes, it began to fog in again.

It was a perfect day. We hiked up and back down the same day for a total of 6.6 miles. We then did a short hike on Sandy Pond Trail. I had my first sighting of a moose feeding in the pond. We sat on the rocks and watched him for a while.

---

[14] History was provided by Baxter State Park Authority's web site at www.baxterstateparkauthority.com/hiking/thru-hiking.html.

We drove to Daicey Pond Campground the second day and hiked the AT south to Big Niagara Falls and back. From there, we drove to Abol Campground and hiked up to Little Abol Falls. We then hiked around Daicey Pond Loop Trail, which includes a portion of the AT.

When we got back to camp, the worst storm I have ever seen came up. We sat in our car for almost two hours until the storm let up. We found out the next day that someone had been struck by lightning and did not make it. He was sitting under a tarp, on the picnic table by the shelter when lightning hit the tree and traveled through the tarp, down to the picnic table. His brother had bad burns to his feet.

We hiked 8.2 miles today.

On the third day, we decided to climb Katahdin. We have tried for two days to climb the mountain, but the weather forecast was not good. Today is our last chance, so we decided to go for it even though there was a 30 percent chance of afternoon thunderstorms.

Rock Stairs at beginning of trail to Katahdin

This is an example of the remarkable rockwork that the volunteers do. Sometimes it will assist us in getting up an almost impossible climb while other times it may just be a way to control erosion or avoid over use to a sensitive ecosystem.

We started out with a cool breeze, but it was overcast with a feel of rain in the air.

You start to get a view of Katahdin Stream Falls as you cross the footbridge. We decided to take a quick break at the falls before the challenging climb up the mountain. From there, you continue to climb along the side of the falls. Charlie and I made good time, and I was surprised at the stamina I had as we continued to climb. I actually enjoyed the challenge of climbing up and over all the boulders. I felt safe with Charlie as my hiking partner. We were almost over the boulder field when a storm started to close in on us. After last night, we decided to turn around and head down the mountain. I never thought I would finish the trail because I had a fear of climbing Katahdin and didn't think I would be able to climb it. I will be back next summer to try again. When we got back to the campground, I met Long Trail, who has been section-hiking for ten years and just now finished his thru-hike. That was the motivation I needed to get started again.

TESTNATEE GAP TO DICKS CREEK GAP, GEORGIA

Spring of 2008

From Testnatee Gap you will traverse a dramatic high ridge via 5 miles of the Appalachian Trail, ending at thru-hiker hangout Walasi-Yi Center.

To trailhead take US 19 north to Georgia 180. Go right onto Georgia 180. Travel east about one mile. Turn right onto Georgia 348 than go about five miles to Testnatee Gap trailhead. Park in lot on right

I decided to go out for a few days to prepare for a ten-day hike at the end of the month with my sister, LaTripper. I hiked this section in 2002 during my long hike. The weather had taken a turn for the worse so I waited one day and left from Testnatee Gap at Georgia Route 348 instead of Neel's Gap.

The climb out of the gap was very strenuous since I hadn't backpacked for a couple of years.

The AT in this section generally follows broad, rocky tops along a well-defined route. From an elevation of 3,138 feet at Testnatee Gap, the trail continues to climb to the top of Wildcat Mountain up to 3,420 feet with an awesome view of Town Creek gorge, bound by the north-south ridges of Cowrock Mountain and Wildcat Mountain to the east.

The only flowers I saw today were fields of mayapple.

The Low Gap Shelter was full tonight and several hikers set up their tents nearby. Gwen and her two daughters, Eli and Stephanie, from Canada are on their way to Maine. Also in the shelter tonight were Matt, Snake Gripper, and his dog, Nova.

This is a nice shelter with a stream running in front of it. Snake Gripper kept a fire going until about 10:00 p.m. It got down into the low thirties last night. I was warm most of the night until about 5:00 a.m. I only hiked for three hours and completed 5.3 miles.

The next morning, I left camp at eight thirty and hiked alone as far as Blue Mountain Shelter. The water is so plentiful in this area. I passed several springs running across the trail in the first few miles out of camp. I stopped for lunch and decided it was too early to stop for the night. Alex, whose trail name is Phexon, said I could hike with him, and we would stop at the old Cheese Factory Site for the night.

In the mid-1800s, an eccentric New Englander established a dairy near Tray Mountain, about fifteen miles from the nearest farmhouse. For several years, the man ran his dairy successfully and reportedly produced a superior cheese that won several awards at state agricultural fairs. Little evidence of the dairy remains today.

Alex "Phexon" at the Cheese Factory Site

The hike up Blue Mountain was very hard for me. From Unicoi Gap, we had a 1,070-foot gain to the top of Rocky Mountain. The views on top made it all worthwhile. I'm starting to see lots of bluetts on the top of the summits now.

We are tucked into the rhododendrons with a wonderful fire. We found wood from a campsite by Tray Mountain Road, USFS Road 79. There is a nice water source on the other side of the road. We retired early since it was beginning to get chilly. I stayed warm with all my layers of clothing on.

About midnight, we heard a car stop on the fire road below our campsite and several men talking loudly as they walked up to the upper campsites. I heard one guy say, "This would be a good place to kill someone." By then, I was shaking from fear. I was very quiet but made sure I knew where my knife was. I only have a small two-inch knife, but I guess that's better than nothing. The men continued to walk down to our sites and I heard them say, "Oh there she is tucked into the woods, and over there is another one. They weren't here last night, and there is no car parked below. Where did they come from? Do you think anyone is inside the tents? Let's get out of here." I heard them leave, and in about five minutes, I heard another car, thinking they were coming back. I asked Phexon if we should move up into the woods, but he reassured me we would be okay. No one bothered us the rest of the night, and I managed to get a good night's sleep.

We hiked 12.9 miles and stopped at the Cheese Factory Site campsites.

We were on the trail by eight this morning. I left ahead of Phexon so I would not slow him down. The climb up Tray Mountain (4,930 feet) was not as hard as I thought it would be. It's very pretty through this section.

We had several ups and downs throughout the day then the climb from hell. Kelly Knob is a one-mile climb without any switchbacks. We went from 3,310 feet to 4,275 feet in one mile. It took me over an hour to climb to the summit, but only twenty minutes to descend one mile into camp. I'm having trouble with my breathing again.

Deep Gap is a nice shelter with two lofts. I set up inside and Phexon, Snake Gripper, and his dog, Nova put their tents up. I decided to move upstairs and hauled all my gear up the ladder and set up for the night. I realized that the shelter had signs of mice so I hauled everything down the ladder and set up down below again. I had just settled into my sleeping bag when I saw two mice come scurrying by. I got up and hauled all my gear outside and began to set up my tent. Phexon got out of his tent and carried all my supplies from the shelter, and Gripper helped me set up. I was settled and snug in my tent within ten minutes, thanks to all the help.

Gripper had hit the trail without any gear to speak of and had just gotten Nova the day he left on his hike. He did not have a stove, sleeping bag, water filter, or much food to last for more than a day or two. I gave him some food and boiled some water so he could cook his rice.

We only hiked 9.5 miles.

Day four was a short three-mile hike to Dicks Creek Gap at US 76 where Ed picked us up and took the guys to Hiawassee, Georgia.

PENNSYLVANIA

May 2008

My sister, LaTripper, and I hiked the section from Pennsylvania 16 north to Duncannon, Pennsylvania. LaTripper had not done this section so I agreed to go out with her. These will be repeat miles for me. Since we were out just after the spring rains, we had plenty of water sources in this section. We met quite a few hikers that had left Springer, Georgia at the end of February. They are hiking twenty-five to thirty miles a day. I don't know how they do it—maybe because they are thirty or more years younger than me.

We had a wonderful hike today. There were not many challenges so we took our time hiking along and enjoying the moment.

We met three guys from Denver, Colorado, the first night at Tumbling Run Shelter. What fun we had listening to all the stories of previous hikes they had done together.

The next day, we took the short trail to Chimney Rocks to the vista and enjoyed the views before continuing on. It was another easy day of hiking with very little elevation gains or losses.

We hiked as far as Caledonia Campground today. When we stopped at the office, we were asked if we would speak tomorrow night at the camp gathering. They were going to be speaking about the Appalachian Trail and women hikers. We agreed and had a great time sharing our stories and inspirations and answering questions. They gave us two free nights and took us out for pizza.

We met two sisters, Vicky and Adrian, Vickie's husband Bobby, and Adrian's friend Robert, who are section-hiking parts of the trail as time allows. They are planning to climb Katahdin in August and invited me to join them. I am considering it.

We left the campground fairly early and got a ride with the Ranger to Pine Grove Furnace State Park. We skipped the section from Caledonia to Pine Grove since we had hiked that before.

If we had brought our bathing suits, we could have spent time at the beach on Fuller Lake. Today was just a walk in the woods. We had very few climbs.

LaTripper and I decided to set up our tents down below the shelter. When we heard thunder in the distance, I decided to pack up my tent and moved to the shelter. LaTripper was going to stay down below but was lonely all by herself so she also moved to the shelter but left her tent set up with all her extra gear in it. We crammed nine hikers into Alex Kennedy Shelter that night, and I think it was the worst night's sleep I have ever had.

The next day, we hiked as far as Boiling Springs. It was another beautiful hike with few challenges. We set up our tents in the backyard of the Garmanhaus Bed and Breakfast for a small fee.

We were crossing roads most of the day. This area is too rural for me. I like to be further away from civilization when I am hiking. An easy day of hiking brought us to the Darlington Shelter for the night.

The following day, we hiked into Duncannon. It was another easy day except for the scramble across the rock slide. We had awesome views of Duncannon from the top. After lunch and a beer at the Doyle Hotel, we rented a car and drove back to LaTripper's house.

This is the third time I have hiked this area. I hope to have a more challenging hike next time out and plan to hike some sections I have not done before.

BAXTER STATE PARK AND KATAHDIN

August 2008

The climb up to Baxter Peak, Katahdin, is the single biggest climb of the entire AT, more than four thousand feet of elevation change to reach the 5,267-foot summit. The ascent will take three to four hours.

We started out on a very rainy morning and hiked the entire day in rain, wind, and fog. When we came to the tree line about halfway up the mountain, we were hoping for a view of the valley below only to be in dense clouds. At this point of the trail, the path enters a field of boulders strewn on the mountainside.

On this slope, iron rungs project from rock faces to give holds for hand and foot.

You then pass through the Gateway and onto The Tableland, a broad, tilted plateau sandpapered by the continental glacier that extends south and west for a mile and north for three more miles.

Less than two miles of walking remained.

Near the trail here, you pass Thoreau Spring. This section of the trail was ankle deep in water from all the rain. I gave up trying to keep my feet dry and just stomped through the water.

The steepest part of the climb was behind us, but we had the final climb up to the summit. I was worn out by this time and was having a problem with my breathing. Robert was kind enough to stay with me on the final summit up.

It was raining most of the day, but it stayed much cooler than if the sun had been out. We did not have any views at the top, but I was just so glad to be there I didn't even mind. It took us six hours to climb up and another six to come back down. I think we could have completed the entire climb in ten hours if it hadn't been so wet and slippery.

What a feeling of accomplishment it is to be at the top and share the excitement of the thru-hikers as they summit the mountain. Some have tears of joy while some rush up to the sign and kiss it. Several hikers told me that the climb up Katahdin was the hardest part of the trail for them. It gave me encouragement to pursue my dreams of completing the trail. I never thought I could climb this mountain; therefore, I could never complete the trail. I now have renewed hope of someday completing the entire Appalachian Trail.

The trip pushed me to the edge of my comfort zone, propelling me to a place I wasn't sure I wanted to be. Even though it was only a little over five miles up, it was more than I ever expected and the hardest thing I have ever done. I don't think I could have done the hike alone and was fortunate to have four other hikers go up with me. The group that we hiked with left the next day to complete seventy miles of the One-Hundred-Mile Wilderness.

Paralee "Trapper Lee" on Katahdin

NEW YORK, CONNECTICUT, MARYLAND, AND PENNSYLVANIA

May-August 2009

My grandson Tyler is very involved with the Scouts and Young Marines. I will have the pleasure of hiking with him all summer. He has been through survival training with the Young Marines and can probably teach me a thing or two. In 2013 he enlisted in the Army and found out he was going to be a daddy just prior to leaving for boot camp.

Well here we go again—the beginning of the longest, most challenging summer of my life. The odds were against me from day one. Well, don't let me get ahead of my story.

It was a joy to be outside and on the trail again. I had struggled with winter, counting the days until I could take my first steps along the Appalachian Trail again.

Ed and I left Murphy, North Carolina the beginning of June for trail days in Damascus, Virginia. I wanted to be a part of the hiker camaraderie, and I also wanted to see if I could sell my book while there. My book sales were very good, and Ed and I enjoyed our final days together until October. He was heading for Maine, and I was going back on the trail with my grandson Tyler Towns.

From Damascus, I drove to my daughter's house in Jacksonville, North Carolina to rest up before I started hiking and to finish getting Tyler's gear together.

I flew to Boise, Idaho to see my oldest grandson graduate and spend time with my son Jeff.

When the day finally came to leave, there were lots of hugs, kisses, and tears as we packed up to go. We drove to Maryland on our way to Kent, Connecticut where I will park my car for the first week of our hike.

We arrived in Kent at three in the afternoon and had two hours to wait for our shuttle to Bear Mountain Bridge, New York. Greg "Ridge Runner" Peters is an avid hiker and goes out each year to hike another section of the Appalachian Trail. He is retired from the Connecticut Department of Corrections and was a Master Sergeant in the US Army. He will shuttle hikers in most of New York, Connecticut, and Massachusetts. His email is ridgerunner@optonline.net, and his phone number is 860-307-7121.

It took us over an hour to reach the hotel. As I was emptying the car, I realized I had left my hiking boots in my car back in Kent. All I had was the Crocs I was wearing. Driving back to Kent was out of the question. Greg sensed my concern and offered me a pair of boots he had in the trunk. They were Merrill, size nine and fit me well. I did not have much cash on me so Greg suggested I just send him a check when I got home at the end of summer.

As if forgetting my boots wasn't enough, I faced another dilemma after dinner when I found out that my debit card would not go through. When I am hiking I don't carry much cash, and I knew I had plenty of funds in the account. I tried calling the bank, but it was after hours. I had enough to pay for dinner, but that only left me with forty dollars in cash. I usually carry a credit card but chose not to this trip. I later found out that my bank had blocked my account because of the large purchase at REI on the way to Maryland.

We got a shuttle from the hotel to Bear Mountain Bridge the next morning where we would take our first steps on the Appalachian Trail. As we approached the bridge, I sensed the lack of enthusiasm I normally have at being on the trail. I had a feeling of worry hanging over me. I usually am so carefree on my hikes and tend to leave my worries at home. I thought maybe it was the added responsibility of having a fifteen-year-old with me. It was so much fun crossing the bridge.

We had a steep climb from the bridge, but we flew up as if we had been hiking for the last month. We took the side trail to Anthony's Nose and enjoyed the views before heading on.

We stopped at the Graymoor Spiritual Life Center for the night. I always wanted to see the Monastery so we only completed 6.4 miles today.

Graymoor is the home of the Franciscan Friars of the Atonement and birthplace of the Christian Unity Movement in America. Thru-hikers have been welcomed here for decades. In past years, hikers stayed in the rectory building and were treated to sumptuous meals with the staff, but those options are no longer available.

Hikers now use the campsite shelter at the ball field, with water, cold shower, and covered picnic pavilion free of charge. We decided to put up our tents as the pavilion began to fill up with hikers. We thought we would have a quiet evening until the hikers decided to build a camp fire and party until 1:00 a.m. Some of the hikers stopped at the Mountain Top Market, which is in view as you cross NY 52. They sell sandwiches, subs, ice cream, and cold drinks including beer. They have a public telephone, water spigot, and a pizzeria next door. Some of the hikers brought beer to the shelter. That night was the beginning of a very long spell of rain.

The second day was hard on both of us. Our energy was low, and Tyler felt like he was coming down with something. The climbs were moderate, but we both seemed to be struggling.

We hiked 8.1 miles and detoured to Dennytown Camp for the night.

We found a nice grassy spot with a picnic table and set up for the night. About one thirty, I started hearing thunder. It continued to get closer, and I knew we were in for a significant storm. We were camped on top of a knoll out in the open field so I was concerned about the lightning. I woke Tyler up and told him to put his rain gear on that there was a chance we would have to seek shelter further down the hill. We headed for the woods, trying to avoid the poison ivy along the edge of the woods. We hunkered down through the storm only to realize our rain gear was not waterproof. We were soaked to the skin and getting very chilled. When the storm finally let up, we started to head back to our tent only to realize we were heading away from camp. Tyler said, "Gram, we're going downhill. Shouldn't we be going uphill?" I was surprised how quickly you can get disoriented in the woods. We made it back without incident and settled in for the rest of the night.

The third day started with the sun shining, but that did not last very long. My feet were chewed up from the boots, and I had a huge blister on my heel. My body was not up to the energy level I was used to. It was a short day, but I was tired. We decided to call it a day and detoured to Clarence Fahnestock State Park. It was a pretty hike up the road along the lakes, but I was so tired I did not enjoy the hike in. Thru-hikers can stay here for free and have access to the bathrooms with showers. We set up camp just in time before the next storm hit. We sat it out in the bathroom and decided to retire early.

We both woke up tired, sore, and sick of the rain. I let Tyler sleep in and we decided to shuttle back to Kent and get my car. I did not have phone range but was able to use the phone at the office and called Greg to see if he was available for a shuttle back to Kent. He gave us a ride, but we had to wait at camp all day until he got off work.

We finally made it back to Kent and decided we needed a good dinner only to realize my card still had a hold on it. After I paid for dinner, I was down to twenty dollars. We did not have enough money to get a hotel room, and I did not know where we could camp. I told Tyler we may have to spend the night in the car. We drove out to Kent Falls for a quick view, and some locals told us to try the Housatonic Meadows Campground up the road. We drove to the Campground and paid for two days. We decided to wait here for my sisters who were joining us for two weeks. Tyler had money so he paid for the two days.

I went to Kent the following morning and got my debit card released.

We ran into Lucky, a hiker we had met on our first night, and invited him to join us at the campground for the night. The Housatonic River was at flood stage, and by morning, we were all sitting in a mud p. We do have bathrooms nearby and a place to clean up.

Lucky rode to Torrington for some needed supplies, and Tyler and I got a larger tent to have somewhere to spend the rainy days while we were waiting for my sisters to arrive.

We found out that a sixteen-year-old had fallen into the river while trying to rescue his friend and was missing. He was found three days later but did not make it. The rain never stopped for the next three days.

We did a few day hikes and went exploring in the rain. Since we were sitting in a mud hole, we decided to move up to the grassy field before my sisters arrived.

My sisters met us on the third day. They set up a large tent to avoid being confined in a small one-man tent only to find out that it was not waterproof. We came back from a rainy hike to find the tent flooded along with the sleeping bags and everything else. We went to Torrington to get them another tent.

We extended our stay at the campground, hoping the rain would let up. We hiked along the AT and looped back to camp on a blue blazed trail. Sometimes, we would take two cars to shuttle back after we completed a section of the trail. We were able to complete the remaining miles of New York and hike as far as Kent into Connecticut.

I didn't think the rain was ever going to let up so we have decided to head for Maine. We stopped for the night to visit with Ed in Rockport, Maine and left the next morning for Baxter State Park. We checked into the Penobscot Outdoor Center for five days. We decided to rent a tent platform that had four bunks. Well, it leaked, and things got wet. We moved to another one that leaked but not as bad. I don't think I will ever be dry again.

The next day, we had a small break in the rain so we decided to go kayaking on the lake where we were camping. LaTripper decided to share a canoe with my sister Janeen. She was not sure how to get into the canoe, and the next thing I heard was her screaming as she was stretched out with her feet in the boat and holding onto the dock. Janeen fell out as she tipped the boat later to find out that the waters were filled with leeches. When we finally worked it all out, we spent several hours out on the lake. We saw a moose feeding on the shore line. What a treat that was.

We went into Baxter, and we all decided to hike up to Katahdin. LaTripper dropped off shortly after Katahdin Stream Falls. Of course, it was raining the whole time. The Trail is quite narrow as you get closer to the boulder field so the water was running down the trail like a river. The water was up to my ankles at times. I was determined that I would not be the one to say turn around. Tyler finally said, "Let's go back."

I was feeling quite ill by the third day so I stayed at camp while they went hiking in Baxter. They hiked around Daisey Pond and encountered a moose in the trail. Tyler just stood his ground and remained quiet. I think he was remembering the instructions: "What to do if you encounter a bear." Janeen had photos of the moose, but she accidentally deleted them. I slept the entire day.

We packed up the next day to head back to Rockland. Since I was still feeling ill, Tyler and I decided to stay with Ed until I felt better. My sisters were going to head back to Pennsylvania from the campground. When I returned to Rockland, I decided to get checked out in the emergency room.

I found out that I had ehrlichiosis, which is from the bite of the lone star tick. It can take five to ten days before you start noticing symptoms. That might explain the lack of energy in the early days of my hike. I was on antibiotics for twenty-one days. It is still raining every day, so Tyler and I decided to head to Pennsylvania and Maryland. We completed some hikes in Pennsylvania, Maryland and West Virginia.

Health and First Aid

Generally, the trail is a safe place. Remember that common sense and foresight are your best allies, and preparation is the key for a healthy trip.

If you are hiking alone, say you are with a larger group. Most of the women I have spoken with said they felt uncomfortable backpacking alone. I have always had the fear of an incapacitating injury

Trust your own intuitions. The odds of something bad happening to you are hundreds of times greater in an urban setting than they are in the wilderness.

Leave your trail name and itinerary with someone.

Camp away from the roads, and don't tell strangers where you plan on camping. Most of the shelters have been moved away from a road access.

Report any incidents of harassment to local law enforcement authorities.

Carry a whistle to use if you are immobile and need help.

Most wounds on the trail will be minor cuts, scrapes, and blisters.

FIRST AID SUPPLIES

- Band-Aids—several sizes
- Steri-Strips or butterfly closures
- Adhesive tape or duct tape
- Moleskin in various sizes or Second Skin
- Sterile gauze pads in several sizes
- Elastic bandage to wrap a sprained ankle or knee
- Needle for splinters or blisters
- Tweezers
- Tube of antiseptic first-aid cream
- Non-aspirin pain reliever
- Neosporin or another antibiotic ointment
- Personal medications as necessary
- Bug repellent and anti-itch ointment
- Eye drops
- Toothbrush and toothpaste
- Nail clippers
- Hand sanitizer
- Toilet paper

BUGS, TICKS, AND SPIDERS

If you're lucky enough to have a breeze, you probably won't have a problem with the bugs. Stop for lunch on a ridge so you can get a breeze while you're resting. Bright colors attract mosquitoes. I guess that is why all our camp clothes are usually in those boring earth tones. The smoke from your campfire will keep the bugs away from the shelter at night. The best defense is to wear long sleeves and long pants and set up your tent early in the evening. I use a mesh head net while I am cooking my dinner.

Spiders don't typically attack people. They only bite if provoked. Check your clothing and boots before getting dressed in the morning. The privies are good hiding places for spiders. If you think a venomous spider has bitten you, send someone for help immediately.

Check for ticks several times a day if you are hiking in the summer months. Wearing light-colored clothing makes ticks easier to spot. I usually tuck my pants into my socks if I am hiking in high grass or weeds. If you find a very small tick, about the size of a pinhead, it most likely is a deer tick. Deer ticks can transmit Lyme disease. If you are bitten, you will probably notice a bulls-eye rash at the site of the bite. Some of the symptoms are fatigue, muscle and joint pain, sore throat, and fever. You should seek treatment immediately.

SNAKES

The rattlesnake and the cottonmouth are common along the trail in the southern states. You should take extreme caution where you sit or walk while in rocky terrain. Snakes like to sun themselves on rocks during the heat of the day. If you should get bitten, and you experience a stinging pain or severe burning around the bite, seek medical help immediately.

ANIMALS

To discourage animals visiting your campsite, it is a good idea to hang food well out of reach. Porcupines, mice, chipmunks, skunks, and squirrels are common in most of the states along the trail. They are very destructive to shelters and personal gear. I usually hang my toiletries with my food bag at night.

You may spot a bear feeding in the morning or early evening. Usually, if they see you, they will take off. Always keep a clean camp and hang your food. Don't sleep in the clothes that you cook in. Hang your cooking utensils with your food. I had three bear encounters while I was out on the trail, and each time, the bear took off within seconds of seeing me. It is so rewarding to be a part of the natural environment.

WATER

Always filter or treat your water. You don't want to get Giardia. It is a disease-causing organism that may be present in clean-looking water. It is spread by fecal contamination of the water supply.

You can boil your water, use mechanical filtration, or use a chemical treatment as an alternative measure of treating water.

LIGHTNING

The odds of being struck by lightning are low, but an open ridge is not place to be during a thunderstorm. Tents are not a safe place to be in. Avoid tall structures such as power line towers, tallest trees, solitary rocks, or open hilltops. Take shelter in a stand of smaller trees or in the forest. Avoid clearings. If caught in the open, crouch down on your pad or roll into a ball.

Summer is the peak season for one of the nation's deadliest weather phenomena— lightning. But don't be fooled, lightning strikes year round.

Hundreds of people are **permanently** injured each year. People struck by lightning suffer from a variety of long-term, debilitating symptoms, including memory loss, attention deficits, sleep disorders, chronic pain, numbness, dizziness, stiffness in joints, irritability, fatigue, weakness, muscle spasms, depression, and more. Lightning is a serious danger. Please don't take it lightly.

General Information

The following resources were very helpful in the planning stages and during my time on the trail.

National organizations such as Appalachian Trail Conservancy, The American Hiking Society, and the Sierra Club are good sources for trail updates or annual events in the area. All of these have local chapters in most of the states you will hike through.

Check with the Chamber of Commerce or an outfitter in your area for organized hikes. You may want to do a few outings to see if long-distance hiking is what you are looking for.

Another way to get the feel of the trail and meet other hikers who share your dreams is to volunteer for trail maintenance along the AT.

I will never presume to be an all-knowledgeable reference for thru-hikers but rather an information resource.

Some of the most valuable information you will find will be at some of the annual events along the east coast, starting with the Appalachian Trail Kick Off (ATKO), held March each year in Dawsonville, Georgia at the Amicalola Falls Lodge. You don't want to miss this one. You can partake in the pack shack down and allow some of the professionals to critique your gear before ever hitting the Trail.

SUGGESTED READING AND RESOURCES

DATA BOOKS, MAPS, AND ONLINE SHOPPING

Appalachian Trail Thru-Hikers' Companion
Published by AT Conservancy, Harpers Ferry, West Virginia

Appalachian Pages
Written and published by David "Awol" Miller

Appalachian Trail Data Book
Published by AT Conservancy, Harpers Ferry, West Virginia

State-by-State Appalachian Trail Guides
Published by the Appalachian Trail Conservancy and the State Maintaining Clubs

Trail Maintaining Clubs have websites that offer a wealth of information about their section of the trail.

National Park Services

USDA Forest Service, Public Affairs Office

EBay is a great source for used or new gear. I found several items at this site when I was gearing up for my long hike.

MAIL DROPS

I prepared twenty-one mail drops, or care packages, prior to leaving for the trail. This is quite an undertaking and requires meticulous planning. Use your guidebooks to estimate how many miles you need to travel before you can replenish your supplies, that is, before you can hike to town, or catch a ride there, to pick up your mail. Then decide how long it will take you to walk that many miles. You have to plan miles per day by assessing distances between shelters, water sources, elevation changes, and many other variables.

Each drop included food with one extra day to take us through to the next town day, along with any personals we thought we might not be able to find in town. Most places will hold your mail for up to thirty days. Check the data books for phone numbers and location updates. I also mailed a bounce box that had all the extras you don't want to carry with you, such as shampoo and personal items.

Mailing Tips

- Repackage your food. I used a lot of Ziploc bags. Take a few extra for your trash.
- Make sure you put "Hold for AT Hiker" and estimated time of arrival on the box.
- Make sure you put "Hold for AT Hiker" and estimated time of arrival on the box. Most places will hold up to thirty days.
- If you should run short of supplies, you can usually find a few items in the hiker boxes. I often left things I didn't need for others.

MY MAIL DROPS ALONG THE TRAIL

- The Blueberry Patch Hostel, Gary Poteat, 5038 Highway 76 East, Hiawassee, GA 30546
- Nantahala Outdoor Center, 13077 Highway 19 West, Bryson City, NC 28713
- The Hiker Inn, Highway 28, Box 5, Fontana Dam, NC 28733
- Mountain Mama's Kuntry Store, 1981 Waterville Rd., Newport, TN 37821
- Uncle Johnny's Nolichucky Hostel, 151 River Road, Erwin, TN 37650
- Kincora Hostel, 1278 Dennis Cove Road, Hampton, TN 37658
- Mount Rogers Outfitters, 110 Laurel Avenue, Damascus, VA 24236
- General Delivery, Pearisburg, VA 24134
- General Delivery, Waynesboro, VA 22980
- General Delivery, Harpers Ferry, WV 25345
- General Delivery, Boiling Springs, PA 17007
- General Delivery, Port Clinton, PA 19549
- General Delivery, Unionville, NY 10988
- General Delivery, Bear Mountain, NY 10911
- Appalachian Mountain Gear, 684 S. Main Street, Great Barrington, MA 01230
- General Delivery, Dalton, MA 01226
- General Delivery, Killington, VT 05751
- General Delivery, Glencliff, NH 03238
- General Delivery, Gorham, NH 03581
- General Delivery, Caratunk, ME 04925

Gear, Equipment, and Food

Your gear doesn't get you to Katahdin. Of course, if you aren't going to Katahdin, the same rule still applies for wherever you are going. Your motivation and determination get you there. Don't sweat the gear as much as those two things. Saving some money from gear to have money for good food and hostels might just help your attitude and improve your chance of success.

Backpacking requires you to be totally self-sufficient. You don't have a car to transport your belongings or a house to come back to at night. Whether you spend one night or a hundred nights hiking and sleeping outside, you can consider yourself a backpacker.

I decided to include my gear list as a reference only. Technology is always improving the gear available to hikers so I'm sure you will adjust my list considerably. Today's fabrics weigh less and allow for less clothing. Avoid cotton. Once it gets wet, it will take a long time to dry and will add unwanted weight to your pack.

Use the three-layer system when purchasing or packing, for a long distance hike:

The first layer is the undergarment and should be a material made to transport moisture away from the body.

The second layer should be synthetic, fleece, or down sweater to provide warmth as it wicks the moisture away from the body, and it will dry much quicker.

The third layer provides water and wind proofing and will be made of nylon or a waterproof breathable fabric.

Buy stuff-sacks in various colors. It makes finding things in your pack much easier.

HIKING BOOTS

Take care of your feet. Make sure you have boots that fit you properly. Check your feet regularly and treat blisters immediately.

I bought two pairs of Lowa high-tops with Vibram soles and Gore-Tex for waterproofing. Break both pairs in before you start the Trail. Usually, one pair won't hold up for six months on the trail.

A boot should feel roomy and comfortable. If one of your feet is larger than the other, fit the boot to the larger foot; you can fill the space around the smaller foot by adding an extra insole. Your heel should be snug but not tight. You should be able to slide your finger between your heel and the back of the boot. Wriggle and curl your toes. If you don't have enough toe room, you may have some very painful descents. Wear your new boots as much as you can before a trip, allowing at least a month to break them in.

BACKPACK AND WATERPROOF PACK COVER

I purchased a Kelty Yosemite 5300 pack, which weighs 5 lbs., 3 oz., for $115.00. Several years later I switched to a Gregory, Baltora 70, which was lighter but still not considered an ultra-light pack. The outfitters recommended a 5,000-6,000 cubic-inch pack for long-term hiking. Make sure to purchase a pack cover that will fit your pack.

You should have a professional fit your pack to your frame size. Cinch the hip belt, and make sure it is resting on your hipbones, not on your waist. The shoulder straps should wrap comfortably around your shoulders. Adjust the load lifter straps, and bring the weight of your pack closer to your body. Clasp the sternum strap across your chest.

Your loaded pack, including food, should weigh between one-fourth and one-third of your body weight. My first pack felt comfy once I got going, but I had never been happy with it. With full winter gear, I can fill it up, but in the summer, I have excess space. The cap does not come off, which would help for summer hiking. I love my Gregory but would like to go even lighter.

SLEEPING BAG, COMPRESSION SACK AND MAT

I had two sleeping bags. I started with a thirty-degree bag and switched to a lighter weight one as I approached summer. I selected a synthetic bag instead of down filler. I upgraded my sleeping bag to a North Face, Chrysalis, fifteen-degree, 600+ goose-down bag. It weighs just less than three pounds. It weighs less than my thirty-degree bag. As I am getting older, I feel the cold more so I will use this bag often.

I have a liner that will add an additional ten degrees to my bag, or I can use it alone on those really hot nights. Never buy a sleeping bag without laying it on the floor and climbing in to test the fit.

A compression sack is optional and adds a small amount of weight but will help compress your sleeping bag down and allow more room in your backpack.

A good sleeping pad is crucial. I used a Therm-a-Rest, but a lot of hikers are using the Z-Rest. I purchased a Big Agnes a few years ago but did not like the noise it made every time I moved at night. It was not a self-inflating mat and I did not like having to inflate it at the end of a tiring hike. I now have a self-inflating REI full length mat. I sleep cold as I get older and needed the extra length.

WATER FILTER

I used a Pur water filter and carried an extra Pur Micro filter. Some hikers use iodine tablets, but I wasn't comfortable using them for an extended length of time. Don't take chances with your water.

Giardia is a microscopic waterborne parasite that causes a prolonged infection. Treating your drinking water is the best way to avoid the parasite. The disease is not normally life-threatening, but its symptoms can be very uncomfortable. Symptoms can last from a week to a couple of months. If you experience fatigue, weight loss, and persistent diarrhea, you should notify your doctor that you might have Giardia. I have recently upgraded to the MSR Sweet Water micro-filter. It is much lighter and easier to use. I am going to purchase the platypus gravity fed back for my next hike. I will enjoy the ease of filtering with this system along with the lighter weight and bulk.

CLOTHING

Below is my list which I have adjusted through the years.

- Rain/wind jacket and pants
- Jacket for colder months
- Down sweater or vest
- Two pairs of hiking pants with zip-off legs
- One pair of shorts for sleeping
- Two long-sleeved shirts
- Two short-sleeved shirts
- Underwear for one week or use panty liners and carry less.
- Two bandanas—one for dishes and one on my pole for sweat.
- Two pairs of socks—one for hiking and one for night time. Never skimp on your socks. They should be a wool-nylon or wool-polypropylene combination. Never wear cotton. Try wearing gaiters to keep your socks dry and to protect your legs. Some hikers will wear sock liners. I did not like them.
- Hat for sun protection—keeps the sun out of your eyes
- Fleece pants

- Gloves (fleece) and a pair of rain-proof mittens (if they get wet, put in sleeping bag overnight or hang with carabineer on backpack)
- Fleece hat
- Long underwear top and bottom made of silk
- Gaiters—I choose not to wear them

FOOD

Some nutritionists recommend that your backpacking diet consist of 70 percent carbohydrates, 15 percent protein, 15 percent fat, and a variety of vitamins and minerals.

Carbohydrates should make up the bulk of your diet. Foods such as pasta, rice, potatoes, oatmeal, fruits, vegetables, crackers, bread, sugars, and honey are good choices.

Protein is essential to help build muscle and provide your body with energy. Foods high in protein include beans, lentils, meat, eggs, cheese, and peanut butter. Eating fat at night will give you energy the next day.

A 128-pound woman will burn 240 to 600 calories per hour while backpacking. If you hike fifteen to twenty miles a day, you will need to consume 4,000 to 4,500 calories a day.

SAMPLE MENU FOR SEVEN DAYS AND SIX NIGHTS

Six Breakfasts
- 3 cups oatmeal and 2 tbsp. brown sugar
- 1 cup dried fruit
- 3 cups granola, with 1 cup powdered milk
- 4 toaster pastries
- 6 tea bags or coffee packets

Seven Lunches
- Energy bars
- 7 cups trail mix
- Half-pound cheese
- Loaf of bread
- 1 cup peanut butter
- 2 soup-mix packets
- 2 flavored pasta packets
- Candy
- 2 cups Gatorade mix

Six Dinners
- A handful of beef jerky
- 3 cups dehydrated potato stew
- 3 cups dehydrated bean soup
- 4 cups macaroni noodles
- 2 chocolate bars
- 3 cups animal crackers
- 1 ½ cups hot chocolate mix
- ½ cup dehydrated sauce

STOVE AND COOKING SUPPLIES

I purchased a Primus Multi-Fuel stove but later converted to an alcohol stove. I love the ease of use and the weight reduction.

A beverage-can is a homemade, ultra-light portable stove. The simple design is usually made entirely from an aluminum can and burns alcohol. Countless variations on the basic design exist.

Total weight, including a windscreen and stand can be less than one ounce (30 grams). The design is popular with backpackers due to its low cost and lighter weight than commercial stoves. This advantage may be lost on long hiking trips, where a lot of fuel is packed, since alcohol has less energy per weight than some other stove fuels. **A stove should never be burned in a tent because even a blue flame produces some carbon monoxide and other poisonous gases.**

Fuel is poured into the stove and ignited, burning in the center. The flame heats the fuel and interior of the stove, causing the fuel to vaporize. When the temperature is high enough, vapor pressure causes fuel jets and a ring of flame.

- Stove stand and wind screen
- Fuel or denatured alcohol and container
- Cook pan—I used titanium since it was lighter. I started with two and found one was sufficient. Instead of a lid use a small piece of aluminum foil.
- Matches or lighter
- Spoon or spork (a combination fork and spoon)
- Biodegradable soap
- Small scrubby to wash dishes with
- Water bottles or containers

TENTING

Tent

I started with the Walrus Zoids 1.0 (this is now the MSR one-man tent) great for hot nights without the rain-fly.

I reduced my weight by purchasing a Big Agnes single man tent. I love the ease of having a free standing tent, but did not like having to crawl into the tent from the end instead of the side.

My third tent was purchased in 2012 and is the LightHeart Solo. LightHeart tents are hiking pole supported shelters utilizing a patent pending support system. This gave me forty-three inches of head room I never had with the previous tents. This tent weighs in at only 27 ounces. If you are traveling with a companion they offer a two man tent with minimal weight. Check it out at www.lightheartgear.com/

Groundsheet

Cut a piece of tyvek or order a footprint from the distributor where you purchase your tent. Some of the hikers choose not to carry one. Keep in mind that a groundcover will protect your investment from ground abrasion and serve as a moisture barrier.

EXTRA SUPPLIES

- Rope
- Sunscreen and lip balm
- Pocket knife
- Rope to hang food—I used parachute cord
- Camp shoes—I used Crocs; they can hang on back of pack when wet and muddy
- Two trekking poles
- Pen and paper
- Carabiner
- Camera (optional)
- Headlamp—I used the Petzl Tikka
- Watch
- Wallet with credit card, cash, phone card, and phone numbers
- Personal items

Every hike I find ways to cut the weight. Talk to other hikers and find out what works for them. They have been my educators. Don't ever skimp on your clothes, hypothermia is a real possibility on top of some of the higher elevations.

Member-Maintaining Clubs

APPALACHIAN TRAIL CONSERVANCY

The Appalachian Trail Conservancy is a private volunteer-based nonprofit organization that is dedicated to the conservation of the Appalachian Trail. The Appalachian Trail Conservancy coordinates planning and management of the trail through the following:

- The assignment of responsibility for sections of the AT to major maintaining organizations.
- The development and publication of trail standards.
- The development of trail management policies.
- Serving as a liaison between the Volunteer Trail Organizations and the National Park Service.

Georgia Appalachian Trail Club (GATC)
P.O. Box 654
Atlanta, GA 30301
(404) 634-6495
www.georgia-atclub.org/about.html

The GATC, based in Atlanta, maintains the southernmost 75.4 miles of the AT from Bly Gap just north of the North Carolina line to Springer Mountain in Georgia, plus the 8.8 mile approach trail from Amicalola Falls State Park.

Nantahala Hiking Club (NHC)
173 Carl Slagle Rd.
Franklin, NC 28734
www.maconcommunity.org/nhc

Franklin, North Carolina-based NHC maintains 58.5 miles of the AT from the Nantahala River at Wesser and U.S. 19 to Bly Gap just north of the North Carolina/Georgia border.

Smoky Mountains Hiking Club (SMHC)
P.O. Box 1454
Knoxville, TN 37901
www.smhclub.org

The Appalachian Trail maintainers committee of the SMHC maintains 102.3 miles of the AT from Davenport Gap, through the Great Smoky Mountains National Park, to the community of Wesser, North Carolina, on the Nantahala River.

Carolina Mountain Club (CMC)
P.O. Box 68
Asheville, NC 28802
www.carolinamtnclub.com

The CMC maintains the AT for the 92.6 miles between Davenport Gap and Spivey Gap. This club is more than eighty years old.

Tennessee Eastman Hiking Club (TEHCC)
Building 310
Kingsport, TN 37662
www.tehcc.org

The TEHCC maintains over 130 miles of the AT and the shelters within from Spivey Gap, North Carolina to Damascus, Virginia.

Mount Rogers Appalachian Trail Club (MRATC)
P.O. Box 789
Damascus, VA 24236-0789

The MRATC was organized in 1960. The club has maintenance responsibilities for fifty-six miles of the trail in the Jefferson National Forest, Mount Rogers National Recreation area, Grayson Highlands State Park, and additional trails in the area.

Piedmont Appalachian Trail Hikers (PATH)
P.O. Box 4423
Greensboro, NC 27404
www.path-at.org

PATH now has responsibility for seventy miles of the storied AT. PATH's maintenance starts from Virginia State Route 670 at the south fork of the Holston River north to US 52 near Bland. This section includes six shelters including the shelter on Chestnut Ridge overlooking the historic and picturesque Burkes Garden.

Outdoor Club of Virginia Tech (OCVT)
P.O. Box 538
Blacksburg, VA 24060
www.outdoor.org.vt.edu

The Outdoor Club at Virginia Tech, based in Blacksburg, Virginia, maintains 27.3 miles of the trail divided into two sections: Pine Swamp Branch Shelter to U.S. 460 at the new River, and Virginia 611 to Interstate 77.

Roanoke Appalachian Trail Club (RAT)
P.O. Box 12282
Roanoke, VA 24024
www.ratc.org

RATC maintains about 121.2 miles of the AT from Blackhorse Gap on the Blue Ridge Parkway south to Pine Swamp Branch Shelter and from Pearisburg at the New River south to Virginia 611 in Bland County.

Natural Bridge Appalachian Trail Club (NBATC)
P.O. Box 3012
Lynchburg, VA 24503
www.nbatc.com

The Natural Bridge Appalachian Trail Club, based in Lynchburg, Virginia, maintains 90.6 miles of the trail from the Tye River at Virginia 56 to Black Horse Gap along the Blue Ridge Parkway.

Tidewater Appalachian Trail Club (TATC)
P.O. Box 8246
Norfolk, VA 23503
www.tidewateratc.org

Based in Norfolk, Virginia, TATC maintains 10.5 miles of the trail from Reed's Gap at Virginia 664 near Wintergreen Resort to Virginia 56 at the Tye River.

Old Dominion Appalachian Trail Club (ODATC)
P.O. Box 25283
Richmond, VA 23260-5283
www.odatc.org

The ODATC maintains 19.1 miles of the AT from Rockfish Gap at the southern end of Shenandoah National Park, near Interstate 64, to Reed's Gap at Virginia 664.

Potomac Appalachian Trail Club (PATC)
118 Park St. SE
Vienna, VA 22180
www.potomacappalachian.org

The Potomac Appalachian Trail Club, based in Northern Virginia, maintains 239.8 miles of the AT from Pine Grove Furnace State park in Pennsylvania to Rockfish Gap near Interstate 64 at Waynesboro, Virginia. PATC has five chapters in the mid-Atlantic region.

Mountain Club of Maryland (MCM)
7923 Galloping Circle
Baltimore, MD 21244
www.mcomd.org
(410) 377-6266

Based in Baltimore, Maryland, MCM maintains two AT sections in Pennsylvania: 12.7 miles south of the Susquehanna River to the Darlington/Tuscarora Trails crossing and the 16.4 miles from Center Point Knob to Pine Grove Furnace State Park at Pennsylvania 233. MCM also maintains the most northern 10 miles of the AT in Maryland.

Cumberland Valley Appalachian Trail Club (CVATC)
P.O. Box 395
Boiling Springs, PA 17007
www.cvatclub.org/home

Based in Boiling Springs, PA, CVATC maintains 17.2 miles of the AT.

York Hiking Club (YHC)
2684 Forest Road
York, PA 17402
(717) 244-6769
www.yorkhikingclub.com

Based in York, Pennsylvania, YHC maintains a 7.2-mile section of the AT from Pennsylvania 225 at the top of Peters Mountain to the Susquehanna River.

Susquehanna Appalachian Trail Club (SATC)
120 Kock Lane
Harrisburg, PA 17112
(717) 657-8281
www.satc-hike.org/

SATC maintains twenty miles of the AT from Rausch Gap Shelter west of Pennsylvania 443 to Pennsylvania 224 north of Harrisburg.

Allentown Hiking Club (AHC)
P.O. Box 1542
Allentown, PA 18105-1542
www.allentownhikingclub.org

Based in Allentown, Pennsylvania, AHC maintains 10.3 miles of the trail, from Bake Oven Knob Road near Pennsylvania 309 (about thirty miles northwest of Allentown) to Tri County Corner.

Blue Mountain Eagle Climbing Club (BMECC)
P.O. Box 14982
Reading, PA 19612-4982
(610) 326-1656
www.bmecc.org

The Reading, Pennsylvania based Blue Mountain Eagle Climbing Club maintains 61.2 miles of the trail, from Lehigh Furnace Gap to Bake Oven Knob Shelter, south of I-81 near Pennsylvania 443.

Philadelphia Trail Club (PTC)
2142 Bristol Road
Warrington, PA 18976-1514
http://m.zanger.tripod.com/

The Philadelphia Trail Club maintains 10.3 miles of the AT from Little Gap, near Danielsville to Lehigh Furnace Gap near Ashfield, Pennsylvania.

Appalachian Mountain Club
Delaware Valley Chapter (AMC-DV)
1180 Greenleaf Dr.
Bethlehem, PA 18017
www.amcdv.org

The AMC-Delaware Valley Chapter maintains 15.4 miles of the trail from Wind Gap at Pennsylvania 33 to Little Gap near Danielsville, Pennsylvania.

The chapter is a part of the larger AMC community of over ninety thousand members throughout the northeast.

Batona Hiking Club (BHC)
6651 Eastwood St.
Philadelphia, PA 19149
www.batonahikingclub.org/
The Batona Hiking Club of Philadelphia maintains 8.6 trail miles from Fox Gap at Pennsylvania 191 to Wind Gap at Pennsylvania 33.

Wilmington Trail Club (WTC)
P.O. Box 1184
Wilmington, DE 19899
www.wilmingtontrailclub.org
The Wilmington Trail Club, based in Delaware, maintains 7.2 miles of the AT from the Delaware River at the New Jersey/Pennsylvania border to Fox Gap at Pennsylvania 191.

New York and New Jersey Trail Conference (NYNJTC)
156 Ramapo Valley Road, Route 202
Mahwah, NJ 07430-1199
(201) 512-9348
www.nynjtc.org/
The NYNJ Trail Conference maintains 160.6 miles of the trail from the Connecticut line to the Delaware River at the Pennsylvania border. The club is based in Mahwah, New Jersey.

Appalachian Mountain Club
www.outdoors.org/
Connecticut Chapter-AMC-CT
(413) 528-6333
www.ct-amc.org/ct/index.htm
The AMC-Connecticut Chapter Trails Committee maintains the 52.3 miles of the trail through the Nutmeg State.

Appalachian Mountain Club
www.outdoors.org/
Berkshire Chapter (AMC-BC)
http://amcberkshire.org/at
964 South Main St.
Great Barrington, MA 02130
(413) 528-6333
The AMC-Berkshire Chapter maintains all 89.5 miles of the AT in Massachusetts from the Vermont line to the Connecticut border

Green Mountain Club (GMC)
4711 Waterbury Stowe Rd.
Waterbury Center, VT 05677
(802) 244-7037
www.greenmountainclub.org/

Based in Waterbury Center, Vermont, GMC maintains 127.9 miles of the AT from Vermont 12 in Woodstock to the Vermont/Massachusetts border near North Adams, Massachusetts. The trail coincides with the Long Trail for 105 miles through southern Vermont.

Dartmouth Outing Club (DOC)
PO Box 9, Hanover
NH 03755
(603) 645-2428
www.dartmoutn.edu/

The Dartmouth Outing Club is a mix of Dartmouth students and local community members around Hanover, New Hampshire. DOC maintains 75.3 miles of the trail from Kinsman Notch at New Hampshire 112 near Woodstock, New Hampshire to Vermont 12 in Woodstock, Vermont.

Appalachian Mountain Club (AMC
5 Joy Street
Boston, MA, 02108
(603) 466-2721
www.outdoors.org/volunteers/index.cfm

The Appalachian Mountain Club maintains 122.2 miles of the trail from Grafton Notch at Maine 26 to New Hampshire 112 in Woodstock, New Hampshire.

Maine Appalachian Trail Club (MATC)
P.O. Box 283
Augusta, ME 04332-0283
www.matc.org

The Augusta, Maine-based Appalachian Trail Club maintains 266.8 miles of the trail in Maine, from Katahdin in Baxter State Park to Grafton Notch at Maine 26.

Saturday, July 25, 2010 was a special day on Katahdin. Seventeen volunteers from throughout New England, and even one from Florida, gathered at Chimney Pond at 9:30 in the morning to carry a new summit sign and framework up the Saddle Trail to Baxter Peak. Temperatures were mild, wind was light from the Northwest, and they were treated to about 15 minutes of sunshine before spending all day in the fog on the mountain.

Volunteers and crew leaders of the Mid-Atlantic Trail Crew are moving stringers into place at Duell Hollow in New York.

Photo by ATC and John Wright

Appalachian Trail Updates

The Appalachian Trail Conservancy is a volunteer-based organization dedicated to the preservation and management of the natural, scenic, historic, and cultural resources associated with the Appalachian National Scenic Trail in order to provide primitive outdoor-recreation and educational opportunities for trail visitors.

The ATC was instrumental in the passage of the federal legislation that designated the AT as America's first national scenic trail in 1968. ATC has been delegated responsibility by the National Park Service to coordinate the management and protection of the trail footpath and its surrounding corridor lands.

ATC works closely with numerous federal, state, and local agencies and with thirty member clubs and their volunteers in the cooperative management of the trail. ATC has close to forty thousand members.

New threats to the trail arise every day. These are threats to a hiking experience and the fragile web of life found on the AT. Even the latest guides and maps can't always keep up with quickly changing trail conditions. Check ATC's website for updates on weather, threats, and relocations along the AT.

The ridge runners record information on water availability, shelter closings, bear activity, and a myriad of information, which can be important to hikers entering the area highways and roads, and planning for appropriate development around the trail corridor.

GREAT SMOKY MOUNTAINS NATIONAL PARK

Permit Fee

In February 2013, the Great Smoky Mountains National Park implemented a new system for obtaining backcountry permits and also began charging fees for permits.

Reduced hours at Post Offices along the A.T

The U.S. Postal Service is cutting hours in many rural post offices, and several along the A.T. will be affected. Those known to have reduced hours already in effect or with proposed cuts to be announced early in 2013 are Suches, Georgia, Fontana Dam, North Carolina, Troutdale, VA, Sugar Grove, VA, Atkins, VA, Montebello, VA, Glencliff, NH, and Warren, New Hampshire and potentially others. For more information, visit www.usps.com. No post offices along the A.T. are expected to close in 2013 during the hiking season.

HURRICANE SANDY IMPACTS

A large swath of the Appalachian Trail was affected by the storm. Trail-maintaining club volunteers have cleared most sections, but areas with heaviest damage may still have blown down trees across the trail. Broken branches may be suspended overhead; be especially careful to look up for potential hazards when pitching camp. A few areas that the Appalachian Trail passes through are still closed or have issued alerts. Check with local agency for closures and more information. Areas that could still be affected:

New York – New Jersey Trail Conference (state parks and forests) www.nynjtc.org and www.nynjtc.org/news/hurricane-sandyrelated-trail-parks-updates.

Portions of the A.T. in Tennessee/North Carolina between Hot Springs and the Great Smoky Mountains National Park have a significant number of downed trees. The latest guides and maps can't always keep up with rapidly changing Trail conditions. Check this page regularly for information on current conditions, relocations, and other big changes along the Trail. More Trail conditions can be found on some local A.T. management partners' websites. If you notice a problem on the Trail, that requires attention, please let the ATC know at trailconditions@appalachiantrail.org.

VANDALISM

Before your hike, be sure to visit the A.T. Shuttle List on the "Parking, Shuttles & Transportation" page for recent vandalism reports in the area you are planning to park your car. Vandalism reports are listed separately at the end of each state's section.

GEORGIA

Post Office Changes - Suches, Georgia
Reduced hours: M - F 9 am - 1 pm. This change took effect Jan. 28, 2013.

Bear canisters seasonally required for camping between Jarrard Gap and Neel Gap.

A new U.S. Forest Service rule requires approved bear-resistant storage containers for overnight camping on a five-mile stretch of the A.T. in the Chattahoochee National Forest between Jarrard Gap and Neel Gap, between March 1 and June 1 each year. This stretch is located between points 26.7 and 31.7 miles north of the southern terminus of the A.T. at Springer Mountain, Georgia, and includes Woods Hole Shelter, Slaughter Creek Campsite, and Blood Mountain Shelter. "Bear canisters" should be used to store food, food containers, garbage and toiletries. For more information, call the Chattahoochee - Oconee National Forest at (770) 297-3000.

NORTH CAROLINA

Long Branch Shelter Open
Construction of the Long Branch Shelter was recently completed by the Nantahala Hiking Club and is now open. It is about two miles north of Albert Mountain in the Nantahala National Forest. There are accessible eating shelves, accessible privy, and the site is laid out with interior trails at accessible grades.

Cold Spring Shelter under construction
The Cold Spring shelter, south of Wesser, NC, is closed while undergoing renovation by the Nantahala Hiking Club.

Post Office Changes - Fontana Dam, North Carolina
Reduced hours: M - F 11:45 am to 3:45 pm. This schedule reflects a change that was implemented during November 2012.

GREAT SMOKY MOUNTAINS NATIONAL PARK

For a full list of road and facility closures and warnings throughout the park, go to **www.atc.org**.

Weather-related road and facility closures may change throughout the day. For updated road and weather information please call 865-436-1200. Once you hear a voice, dial extension 631 for road information or extension 630 for a weather forecast. Since this is one of the most popular parks on the east coast it is recommended you stay up to date on any changes to the rules for hiking through the Smokies. Remember no pets allowed, so if you are hiking with a dog, make arrangements in advance for you hiking companion.

New Backcountry Permit Fees

Starting February 13, 2013, a backcountry permit must be obtained for overnight stays before entering the Great Smoky Mountains National Park, and a $4 per person fee will be required for each night in the backcountry. Backcountry permits can be obtained up to 30 days in advance. Hikers who meet the definition of an Appalachian Trail thru-hiker (those who begin and end their hike at least 50 miles outside the park and only travel on the A.T. in the park) are eligible for a thru-hiker permit of $20 (valid for 38 days from the date issued for an up to 8 day hike through the Park). Permits are available at www.smokiespermits.nps.gov. You may also obtain a permit in person at the park's Backcountry Office (at the Sugarlands Visitor Center near Gatlinburg) or over the phone; with permits issued by fax, mail or email. Hikers staying overnight in the backcountry are required to have a printed copy of the permit.

Newfound Gap Road

Heavy rains have caused flooding and resulted in a landslide that necessitated a closure of Newfound Gap Road (US 441). Rivers and streams have been running fast and high since January 13, 2013 when the rains began. There are currently multiple temporary road closures throughout the park due to high water. The US 441 closure on the North Carolina side (from Newfound Gap to Smokemont) is expected to last an extended period of time, but the Tennessee side from Newfound Gap to Gatlinburg is expected to re-open soon

NORTH CAROLINA & TENNESSEE BORDER

Unaka Mountain Relocation

Volunteers from TEHCC, ATC Konnarock Crew, Hard Core Crew, and student groups recently completed a series of relocations on the north side of Unaka Mountain.

Apple House Shelter Removed

The Apple House Shelter, trail south of 19E between Overmountain Shelter and Mountaineer Shelter, has been removed. The Tennessee Eastman Hiking and Canoeing Club worked with the USFS and ATC to coordinate the removal due to issues with its location and use.

SOUTHWEST VIRGINIA

Grindstone Campground now open

Mt. Rogers - vehicle break-ins and thefts
The Trail between Damascus and VA Rt. 16 at Mt. Rogers NRA Headquarters has a long history of vehicle break-ins and thefts

Post Office Changes - Sugar Grove, Virginia
Reduced hours to take place January 2013: M - F 8:30 am - 12 pm, 2 pm - 4:30 pm; Saturday 8:15 am - 10:30 am. New schedule will take place January 2013.

Post Office Changes - Atkins, Virginia
Reduced hours: Monday through Friday, 8:30 am - 12:30 pm & 1:45 pm -3:45 pm; Saturday 9 am - 10:45 am. This schedule reflects a change that took place Jan. 12, 2013.

Post Office Changes - Bastian and Troutdale, Virginia
Hours expected to be cut; no specific schedule confirmed yet.

CENTRAL VIRGINIA

Va. 621, Craig Creek Valley north to Dragons Tooth
Fire Damage

Fire damage from the February 2011 Pickle Branch Fire may be visible in this area. As always, hikers are encouraged to stay on established trails, particularly in the burned areas.

USFS 35, Petites Gap; Blue Ridge Parkway milepost 71 south to approximately milepost 74.9

Fire damage from the November 2011 Boom Axe Fire may be visible. As always, hikers are encouraged to stay on established trails, particularly in the burned areas

As always, hikers are reminded to follow good Leave No Trace practices and minimize your campfire impacts

Post Office Changes - Montebello, Virginia

These are tentative reduced hours to take effect during 2013 - M - F 10 am - 2 pm.

SHENANDOAH NATIONAL PARK

Little Calf Mountain; Beagle Gap, Skyline Drive mile 96.9 - Relocation opened

The Potomac Appalachian Trail club opened another relocation on Little Calf Mountain, just north of Rockfish Gap. The relocation turns trail west in a field a few hundred yards north of the parking area at Beagle Gap on Skyline Drive, curls around Little Calf Mountain while climbing to its summit, then rejoins the existing A.T. a few hundred yards north of the Little Calf summit.

Temporary relocations due to construction in South District

Several Skyline Drive overlooks in the South District of the Shenandoah National Park will be reconstructed in the spring and summer of 2012. The Ivy Creek Overlook, milepost 77.5, which the A.T. traverses, will be closed for construction from now until further notice. A planned temporary relocation of the A.T. around the overlook is in place. The temp relocation leaves the A.T. approx. thirty yards north and south of the overlook, and follows a route on the west side of Skyline Drive marked by white blazed markers for approx. one-hundred yards. The Horsehead Mountain and Rip Rap Overlooks are sometimes used to access the A.T. as well. Starting in late June or early July those overlooks will be reconstructed and parking will be unavailable for two to three months.

Bearfence Mountain Hut access trail relocated
The access trail to Bearfence Mountain Hut has been relocated from a direct spur from the A.T. to the shelter. It now utilizes two existing woods roads. The old blue blazed access trail has been completely brushed in and access to the shelter now utilizes the yellow and blue blazed Slaughter Trail In one-tenth mile, turn right on blue blazed trail on woods road (yellow blazed Slaughter Trail continues straight ahead, generally downhill). Go one-tenth mile to Bearfence Mountain Hut.

Gravel Springs Gap north to Compton Gap fire damage
Fire damage from the February 2011 Smith Run Fire may be visible in this area. As always, hikers are encouraged to stay on established trails, particularly in the burn areas.

NORTHERN VIRGINIA

Post Office Changes - Bluemont, Virginia
Reduced hours: M - F 10 am - 1 pm, 2 pm - 5 pm; Saturday 8:30 am - 12 pm. This change took place Jan. 12, 2013.

WEST VIRGINIA

Harpers Ferry – side trail to ATC update

Recent construction along the side trail to ATC to make an NPS building handicapped accessible has resulted in a very slight change in the route in the vicinity of Cook Hall (a three-story stone building below the brick Mather Training Center). Some signage and blazing is now obsolete and may not be replaced or updated until spring. Between the A.T. junction and ATC, follow the blue blazes, and take the steep concrete stairway with rails.

MARYLAND

Gathland State Park – Water available

Water is available at Gathland State Park from a spigot by the restrooms, 0.4 south of the Crampton Gap Shelter side trail.

Dahlgren Campground bear activity

Hikers have reported food supplies stolen by a bear at the Dahlgren Backpacker Campground. South Mountain SP has also noted other reports of bear problems in the area. Although black bears have not historically posed much of a problem to hikers in Maryland, they are out there and are now being seen more frequently.

Raven Rock Shelter open

Access to the new shelter is on the west side of the A.T., just a few feet south of the access to the old Devil's Racecourse Shelter. The water source is a spring located three tenths mile east from the A.T. (on the blue-blazed trail to the old shelter on Ritchie Road).

PENNSYLVANIA

Pine Grove Furnace State Park – New parking rules
Pine Grove Furnace State Park requires that hikers check in with the park office before leaving a vehicle in the park and those vehicles be left for no more than one week.

The Ironmasters Mansion hostel - Reopened for business
Note that the doors are locked from 9 a.m. to 5 p.m. daily.

Boiling Springs Parking
The municipal lot by the historic iron forge, which was closed for paving during April and May, 2012, is now open. Hikers must still obtain a permit from ATC's regional office on 4 East First Street (on the A.T.), but there are plenty of parking spaces available.

Rausch Gap Shelter is now open
The Blue Mountain Eagle Climbing Club has completed the shelter renovations and it now open for overnight use.

Hamburg parking is limited
Parking at the end of Reservoir Road is limited due to construction associated with Hamburg Watershed facilities

Lehigh Gap to Little Gap – Remedial & restoration activities in progress
Remedial activities are currently being conducted near the A.T. between Lehigh Gap and Little Gap as part of the Palmerton Zinc Pile Superfund Site. These activities include the re-vegetation of Blue Mountain by applying a mixture of seed, fertilizer and lime, access road construction and improvements, invasive plant control with the use of chemical herbicides, and installation of deer exclusion fence for the establishment of woody species. The Appalachian Trail and blue-blaze Winter Trail will remain open during these activities. For your safety, please stay on the blazed routes.

Post Office Changes - Danielsville, Pennsylvania
Reduced hours: M - F 8:30 am - 12 pm, 2 - 4:30 pm; Saturday 8 am - 12 pm.

Delaware Water Gap Toll Bridge Facility - Construction project
The Delaware Water Gap Toll Bridge Facility will undergo a construction project from January 14 through October 1, 2013. The facility is located on Delaware Avenue, which is part of the A.T. Hikers should be alert to the construction activities and exercise caution. Impact on hikers is expected to be minimal. The sidewalk on the northern side of the street will remain open for the duration of the project and hikers should use that route for passage. The lower section of sidewalk on the southern side of the street will be closed and fenced off.

NEW JERSEY

Delaware Water Gap National Recreation Area road closed
Blue Mountain Lakes Road, which crosses the A.T. about 17 miles north of the Delaware River and is permanently closed east of the trail, remains closed to the west side of it at Old Mine Road. This closure is due to damage to the road from last year's storms.

Sunfish Pond - Relocation opened
From the A.T. - Garvey Springs Trail junction north to a stream near the Upper Yards Creek Reservoir, a distance of about one mile, the trail has been relocated several hundred yards to the west. It now follows a contour just to the west of the height of land of the ridge. Just before rejoining the existing trail, the relocation provides an extensive up-river view of the Delaware River valley

NEW YORK

Post Office Changes - Unionville, New York
Reduced hours: M - F 8 - 11:30 am, 1 - 5 pm; Saturday 8 am - 12 pm.

Little Dam Lake – Little Dam Bridge collapsed
Little Dam Bridge, just south of Little Dam Lake, 3 miles west (or Trail south) of NY 17 and the NY Thruway, collapsed. A crew from the New York-New Jersey Trail Conference has installed step stones.

Post Office Changes - Southfields, New York
Scheduled to change in the spring; no projected hours or date confirmed yet.

West Mountain Relocation

Heading southbound, after crossing Seven Lakes Drive, the Trail meets and is co-aligned with the 1777 W trail for one-tenth mile, then the new route turns left. After another one-tenth mile, the trail meets and turns right on an old woods road. After about two-tenths mile, it turns left off the woods road and climbs for about four-tenths mile, where it rejoins the old A.T. at an open area with good views. The relocation is about one mile, roughly two-tenths longer than the old route.

Bear Mountain Relocation
Parts of a planned three-mile relocation of the A.T. over Bear Mountain have been opened to the public. Hikers should pay close attention to blazing in the area. Work on the remainder of this relocation and restoration of the old route and social trails in the area will continue.

CONNECTICUT

Post Office Changes - Cornwall Bridge, Connecticut
Reduced hours: M - F 8:30 am - 1 pm, 2 pm - 5 pm; Saturday 9 am - 12 pm.

Post Office Changes - Sharon, Connecticut
Reduced hours: M - F 9:30 am - 4:30 pm; Saturday 9:30 am - 12:30 pm.

Guinea Brook (just north of Conn. 4/Cornwall Bridge) – Stepping stones washed away
The rock stepping stones across Guinea Brook are no longer safe to use. Crossing Guinea Brook requires fording or utilizing the blue blazed bypass trail. Use the "high water bypass" or the Mohawk Trail, or continue South on RT 4 to the Breadloaf Mountain parking area and take the blue trail to rejoin AT. The bypass is strongly recommended during periods of high water or icing.

Iron Bridge, Housatonic River - Closed to motor vehicles
The Iron Bridge across the Housatonic River at Fall Village near the power plant has been closed to motor vehicles by the Town of Salisbury. Pedestrian use is allowed at this time, but eventually the bridge will be closed to hikers when renovations begin. A relocation marked by orange blazes, involving a road walk on RT 128 and Dugway Road, will be instituted when the bridge officially closes during construction. September 19, 2012.

MASSACHUSETTS

Upper Goose Pond Cabin Closing

The cabin will be closed for the season on October 21st (last night to stay in the cabin October 20th). After cabin closing hikers may use the open porch or tent platforms to camp as in the past. Hikers are advised to use the bear boxes to store their food as bears are still active. Also, please no cooking on the porch; use the cook table under the pavilion roof behind the cabin.

VERMONT

Post Office Changes - Danby, Vermont

Hours likely to be reduced to six hours each day; no specific schedule confirmed yet.

In September 2011, Hurricane Irene caused damage all along the A.T., but Vermont was hit hardest with extensive damage to the footpath, bridges, and access roads is still being addressed. Some bridges are still out so be careful when crossing streams; river crossings can be deceptively hazardous

The following portions of the Appalachian Trail remain closed with marked detours:

Short relocation around Gulf Stream crossing near Rte. 12
Stony Brook Bridge is out and fording is required
Sargent Brook Bridge, near Governor Clement, is out and fording is required
The LT/AT between Governor Clement Shelter and Sherburne Pass is in rough shape and should be avoided until spring 2013, when the trees are slated to be removed.

NEW HAMPSHIRE

Post Office Changes - Lyme and Wentworth, New Hampshire
Hours likely to change; projected schedule unknown at this time.

Ore Hill Shelter –Burned down
The Ore Hill Shelter, along Dartmouth Outing Club's section burned down sometime in late October 2011. ATC, DOC and Forest Service partners are investigating the cause and local situation. There are no current plans underway to replace it; however, as many A.T. club maintainers know, our system of continuous overnight shelters, lean-tos and campsites requires continuity. ATC will inform the public about the club's and partners' plans as soon as they are known.

Post Office Changes - Warren, New Hampshire

Reduced hours: M - F 7:30 am - 9:30 am and 3 pm - 5 pm; Saturday 7:30 am - 11:30 am. This change took effect Jan. 12, 2013.

Post Office Changes - Glencliff, New Hampshire
Current hours are Monday - Friday 7 am - 10 am; 2 pm - 5 pm; Saturday 7 am - 1 pm. projected hours (tentative) will be 2:30 pm - 4:30 pm Monday through Friday.

Cascade Brook Bridge out
The bridge on the A.T. (also known as the Cascade Brook Trail) over Cascade Brook was washed out during a spring 2011 flood. A short distance upstream from the former bridge site there is a rock hop crossing suitable at low to moderate water levels.

During high water, the rock hop crossing is not safe and hikers should seek alternate routes. Heading northbound: It is recommended to leave the A.T. at Lonesome Lake and take the blue-blazed Lonesome Lake trail to the Pemi Trail (at the Lafayette place campground) and rejoin the A.T. just before going under Franconia Parkway (I-93/NH Rt.3).

Heading southbound: Take the Pemi Trail after going under the Parkway to the Lonesome Lake Trail. See the A.T. New Hampshire-Vermont guidebook and map #3 or AMC's White Mountain Guide and Franconia-Pemigewasset map #2.

MAINE

Post Office Changes - Oquossoc, Maine
Expected to be reduced; no projected schedule confirmed.

Access to Mt. Abraham– the Rapid Stream road damaged
It is being repaired only to the last house which is 3 miles short of the trailhead, the twin bridges are gone too.

Kennebec Ferry Service– 2012 Schedule
May 25 –July 12: 9 a.m. to 11 a.m. only

July 13 – September 30: 9 a.m. to 11 a.m. and also 2 p.m. to 4 p.m.

October 1 – October 8: 9 a.m. to 11 a.m. only

Contact David P. Corrigan, ferry contractor, at (207) 672-4849 for details and current information regarding the ferry service.

Post Office Changes - Monson, Maine
Tentative projected schedule: M - F 8 am - 12 pm, 2:15 pm - 4:15 pm; Saturday 7:30 - 11:00 am. Date to take place not confirmed - likely spring 2013.

Gulf Hagas side trail– Footbridge washed out
The Gulf Hagas Brook Bridge was washed out by spring high water. This does not affect the A.T. itself, but does affect access to a popular side trail. A replacement bridge will likely not be installed until fall (at the earliest). Until the bridge is replaced, hikers using the Gulf Hagas side trail will need to wade across the brook. Please cross at the designated ford rather than trampling brush up and down the banks of the stream.

Baxter State Park – Winter Hiking Season Visit www.baxterstateparkauthority.com for closures and important information.

Katahdin from Chimney Pond Trail
in
Baxter State Park

Lyme disease is a very real thing out on the Trail. Be sure to check yourself every night. Use the buddy system and check each other's backs. My friend found thirty-five ticks on her one night and rushed to the emergency room the next day. They were very lucky and did not contract the disease.

My sister got bit by a tick and acquired Lyme's disease prior to dropping off the Trail. She was in the emergency room and then on antibiotics for ten days. She has had numerous flare ups but seems to be okay the past years.

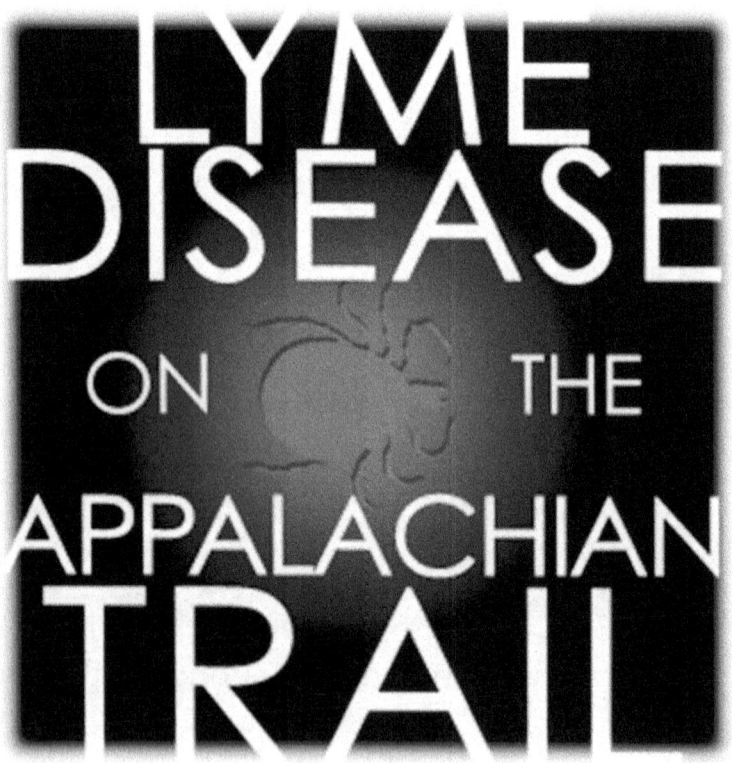

Final Thoughts

When backpacking for weeks, or even months at a time, it becomes a mental challenge more than a physical one. Take time to enjoy your walk in the woods, forget about the miles and getting to the end of the trail. Remember to hike the hike that is right for you. If you never finish hiking the Appalachian Trail, you will still have a lifetime of experiences to share with friends and family.

I have now completed over one thousand six hundred miles of the Appalachian Trail. The sense of accomplishment is overwhelming.

As I leave you, I want to share one final thought with you. Don't be afraid to take chances in life. Live one day at a time, and live it with gusto. Realize your life is truly your life and it belongs to you so when the stormy winds of life threaten to knock you down, have the courage to spread your wings and fly

I found the following inspiration a few years ago and have kept it on my desk ever since.

"Life should not be a journey to the grave with the intention of arriving safely in a pretty and well-preserved body, but rather to skid in broadside, chocolate in one hand, red wine in the other, thoroughly used up, totally worn out, and loudly proclaiming, WOW WHAT A RIDE!

Believe in yourself, there is no limit but the sky if you

**DREAM
DARE
PERSEVERE**

you will succeed!

About the Author

Paralee Dawson-Hayward is a writer of non-fiction, specializing in her adventures along the Appalachian Trail.

She grew up in the country, is one of twelve children, and spent a lot of time in the great outdoors from a very young age. She has always tried to incorporate nature into herself and found hiking or backpacking the perfect way to surround her with the great outdoors.

She started reading the journals of hikers as they traversed the Appalachian Trail and could feel the tug to be part of it all. Her life has been one so few are fortunate to enjoy, one of peace and beauty. She enjoys being a part of people's lives, their future, and their fate. At the age of fifty-seven, she succumbed to white blaze fever and began her exciting hike along the Appalachian Trail. Even in her sixties she is still hiking. Her desire is to bring forth an abundance of inspiration and hope for all those who are about to fulfill their own dreams.

Dawson is the wife of Edwin Hayward and the mother of three children, Patrick, Treasa, and Jeffery. She is a native of New Windsor, Maryland but currently resides in Murphy, North Carolina.

She felt that a book should be a reflection of the author so she decided to take control of all the editorial, designing, and distribution elements and took on the challenges of self-publishing and writing her own book. This was at times more challenging than her hike.

Paralee Dawson-Hayward

Questions for the Author can be e-mailed to
paralee@outdoorhikerbooks.com
www.outdoorhikerbooks.com

A

Abingdon Gap Shelter, 74
Abol Bridge, 24, 161, 162
Alex Kennedy Shelter, 180
Allegheny Mountains, 34, 94
Allen Gap, 61
Allentown Hiking Club (AHC), 209
American Hiking Society, 193
Amicalola Falls, 17, 36, 206
Amicalola Falls State Park, 36, 206
animals, 28, 118, 168, 172, 191
Annapolis Rock, 126, 128
Appalachian Mountain Club, 155, 209, 210, 211
Appalachian Pages, 27, 194
Appalachian Trail, 5, 6, 11, 12, 13, 14, 15, 16, 19, 21, 22, 27, 28, 30, 35, 36, 52, 54, 81, 82, 106, 109, 110, 125, 126, 140, 141, 149, 150, 151, 155, 156, 157, 159, 167, 172, 179, 182, 183, 184, 193, 194, 205, 206, 207, 208, 209, 211, 213, 231, 233
Appalachian Trail Conservancy, 21, 22, 27, 28, 155, 193, 194, 205, 213
Appalachian Trail Data Book, 27
Apple House Shelter, 69
Apple Orchard Falls, 97
Apple Orchard Mountain, 96, 97
Ashby Gap, 119

B

Bailey Gap Shelter, 89
Bake Oven Knob, 141, 209
Bald Mountain, 64, 150
Bald Mountain Shelter, 64
Bald Peak, 150
Batona Hiking Club (BHC, 210
Baxter Peak, 172, 181, 212
Baxter State Park, 172, 173, 181, 187, 188, 211

Bear Mountain, 19, 150, 163, 167, 168, 169, 183, 184, 196
Bear Mountain Bridge, 168
Bears Den, 120
Bears Den Rock, 120
Beauty Spot Mountain, 65
Benton MacKaye, 19, 52
Benton MacKaye Trail, 52
Berkshire Plateau, 151
Berkshires, 21, 151
Big Bald, 63
Big Cedar Mountain, 38
Big Meadows, 112
Big Niagara Falls, 161, 174
Bigelow Preserve, 158
Bill Irwin, 13
Black Horse Gap, 95, 207
Black Rock Cliffs, 128
Blackrock Hut, 108
Blood Mountain, 37, 39
Blue Mountain, 34, 40, 137, 140, 141, 143, 145, 176, 177, 209
Blue Mountain Eagle Climbing Club, 209
Blue Ridge Mountain, 20, 34, 54, 55
Blue Ridge Parkway, 20, 95, 97, 207
Blueberry Knoll Trail, 173
Blueberry Patch Hostel, 41
Bluff Mountain, 100
Bobblets Gap Shelter, 95
Boiling Springs, 132, 180, 196, 208
Bradford Mountain, 150
Brier Knob, 54
Brown Fork Gap Shelter, 50
Brown Mountain Creek Shelter, 101
Bryant Ridge Shelter, 95
Buchanan Mountain, 165
Buttermilk Falls, 146

C

Cable Gap Shelter, 51
Caledonia State Park, 33, 130
Calf Mountain Shelter, 106

Camp David, 128
Camp Ken-Etiwa-Pec, 145
Canaan Mountain, 150
Carolina Mountain Club, 206
Cartecay River, 36
Carver Gap, 68
Catawba Mountain Shelter, 93
Catawba Valley, 94
Cathedral tTrail, 173
Charlie's Bunion, 57
Chatfield Shelter, 81
Chattahoochee National Forest, 22
Cheese Factory Site, 177, 178
Cheoah Bald, 49
Cherokee National Forest, 22
Chestnut Bald, 54
Chestnut Knob Shelter, 84
Chestoa Bridge, 64
Chimney Pond, 173, 212
Chimney Pond Trail, 173
Chimney Rocks, 129, 179
Civil War, 31, 101, 102, 123, 125, 126, 127, 130, 131
Civilian Conservation Corps, 47, 109
Clarence Fahnestock State Park, 186
Clarendon Gorge, 154
Clingman's Dome, 20, 22, 39, 53, 56, 73
Clothing, 200
Clyde Smith Shelter, 67
Cold Mountain, 102
Cold Spring Shelter, 47
Connecticut, 20, 150, 151, 163, 183, 187, 210
Cooking, 201
Coon Den Falls, 70
Cosby Knob Shelter, 58
Cowrock Mountain, 176
Crampton's Gap, 126
Creeper Trail, 75
Crescent Rock, 120
Crissey Ridge, 150
Cumberland Valley, 128, 208
Cumberland Valley Appalachian Trail Club, 208
Curly Maple Gap Shelter, 65
CVATC, 208

D

Dahlgren Backpack Campground, 126
Daicey Pond Loop Trail, 174
Daisey Pond, 188
Daleville, 93
Damascus, 72, 74, 75, 76, 77, 129, 183, 196, 206
Dartmouth Outing Club, 211
David Lesser Memorial Shelter, 121
David Miller, 27
Davis Path Shelter, 82
Deep Gap, 60, 66
Deep Gap Shelter, 41
Delaware Water Gap, 144, 145
Dennis Cove Road, 70, 196
Dennytown Camp, 186
Derrick Knob Shelter, 55
Devil Fork Gap, 62
Devil's Racecourse, 120
Dicks Creek Gap, 41, 176, 179
Double Cap, 161
Double Spring Gap Shelter, 56
Double Springs Gap Shelter, 73
Dover Oak, 90
Doyle Hotel, 133, 180
Dudley Trail, 173
Duncannon, 133, 134, 179, 180

E

Earl Shaffer, 12, 13, 74, 136
Ed Garvey Shelter, 125
ehrlichiosis, 188
Elk Garden Campsites, 77
Ellijay, 36
Emma Caldwell Gatewood, 12
Extra Supplies, 204

F

Fat Man Squeeze Tunnel, 79
First Aid Supplies, 190
Fitzpatrick Falls, 165
Flat Top Mountains, 97
Floyd Mountain, 96
Fontana Dam, 48, 51, 52, 196

Fontana Hilton Hostel, 51
Fort Dietrich Snyder Marker, 137
Fort Montgomery, 168, 169
Franciscan Friars, 185
Franconia Range, 155
Fuller Lake, 31, 180
Fullhardt Knob Shelter, 94

G

GATC, 36, 205, 206
Gathland State Park, 125, 126
Gear, 196, 197
George Washington National Forest, 102
Georgia, 6, 12, 15, 17, 19, 20, 22, 23, 25, 35, 36, 37, 44, 47, 49, 57, 87, 96, 126, 176, 179, 206
Gertrude's Nose, 169
Glass Hollow Overlook, 103
Gooch Gap Shelter, 37
Grandma Gatewood, 12, 13
Grassy Ridge, 68
Gravel Springs Hut, 115
Graymoor Spiritual Life Center, 26, 185
Grayson Highlands State Park, 24, 79, 206
Great Smoky Mountains National Park, 22, 51, 52, 54, 59, 206
Green Mountain Club, 211
Green Mountain National Forest, 22, 152
Green Mountains, 21
Greenbrier State Park, 127
Greenwood Lake, 164, 165, 167
Gridley Mountain, 150
Grindstaff Monument, 72
Groundhog Creek Shelter, 60
Guillotine, 98

H

Hamlin Ridge Trail, 173
Harmon Den Mountain, 60
Harpers Ferry, 20, 29, 30, 116, 118, 120, 122, 123, 151, 155, 194, 196
Harriman State Park, 167
Helveys Mill Shelter, 85

High Falls, 169
Hiker Inn, 196
Hiking Boots, 198
Hog Back Ridge Shelter, 63
Holston River, 83, 207
Hot Springs, 60, 61
Housatonic Meadows Campground, 187
Housatonic River, 150, 187
Housatonic River Valley, 150
Huckleberry Knob, 91
Hudson River, 168, 169
Hughes Gap, 67
Hump Mountain, 69
Humpback Mountains, 105
Humpback Rocks, 103

I

Ice Water Spring Shelter, 56
Iron Mountain, 73
Island Pond, 168

J

James River, 98, 99
Jane Bald, 68
Jefferson National Forest, 79, 206
Jefferson Rock, 123
Jennings Creek, 95
Jenny Knob Shelter, 86
Jerry Cabin Shelter, 62
Jim and Molly Denton Shelter, 118

K

Katahdin, 12, 13, 15, 17, 19, 20, 21, 22, 24, 25, 87, 115, 144, 157, 161, 162, 172, 173, 174, 175, 180, 181, 182, 188, 197, 211, 212
Katahdin Stream Falls, 188
Keffer Oak, 90
Kelly Knob, 41, 90, 178
Kennebec River, 157, 162
Killer Mile, 158
Killington, 152, 196
Kimsey Creek Trail, 45
Kincora Hiking Hostel, 70

Kincora Hostel, 72, 196
Kinsman Range, 155
Knife's Edge Trail, 173
Knot Maul Branch Shelter, 83

L

Lake Tiorati, 168
Laurel Falls, 71
Laurel Fork Gorge, 71
Laurel Fork Shelter, 71
Laurel Top Mountain, 56
Ledyard Bridge, 155
Lewis Mountain, 112
Lick Creek, 83, 84
Lions Head, 150
Little Wolf Creek, 85
Low Gap, 40, 73, 176
Low Gap Shelter, 40, 176
Luray Caverns, 115

M

Mahoosuc Notch, 158
Mahoosuc Range, 21
Mail Drops, 195, 196
Maine, 15, 17, 19, 20, 21, 22, 28, 36, 67, 87, 112, 125, 145, 148, 155, 157, 158, 159, 161, 162, 172, 176, 183, 187, 211
Maintaining Clubs, 194, 205
Manassas Gap Shelter, 119
Margaret's Cliff, 169
Maryland, 13, 20, 35, 119, 123, 125, 126, 127, 128, 143, 148, 183, 184, 208, 233
Massachusetts, 20, 21, 150, 151, 152, 184, 210, 211
MATC, 211
Max Patch, 60, 65
McAfee's Knob, 93, 94
McClure Gap, 179
MCM, 208
Mill River, 153
Mollies Ridge Shelter, 52, 53
Mombasha High Point, 165
Moreland Gap Shelter, 70

Mount Everett, 151
Mount Frissell, 150
Mount Le Conte, 57
Mount Peter, 165
Mount Rogers, 76, 78, 79, 196, 206
Mount Washington, 19, 22, 66, 155
mountain laurel, 60, 80, 89, 93, 129
Mountain Mama's, 57, 59, 60, 196
MRATC, 206
Mt. Greylock, 151
Mt. Mitchell, 61
Murphy, 183, 233
Muskrat Creek shelter, 44

N

Nantahala Gorge, 47
Nantahala Hiking Club, 206
Nantahala National Forest, 22
Nantahala Outdoor Center, 48, 196
National Park Services, 194
National Parks, 22
National Zoological Research Center, 118
NBATC, 99, 102, 207
Neel's Gap, 37, 39, 176
New Hampshire, 19, 20, 21, 22, 66, 67, 97, 155, 156, 211
New Jersey, 20, 145, 147, 163, 210
New River, 88, 207
New York, 19, 20, 90, 145, 146, 163, 165, 166, 169, 170, 183, 187, 210, 212
Newfound Gap, 56
No Business Knob Shelter, 64
North Carolina, 14, 20, 22, 41, 43, 44, 45, 47, 51, 52, 54, 60, 62, 63, 67, 69, 70, 84, 112, 126, 183, 206, 233
NYNJTC, 210

O

OCVT, 207
ODATC, 208
Old Orchard Shelter, 80
One-Hundred Mile Wilderness, 21, 157
One-Hundred-Mile Wilderness, 182

Over Mountain Shelter, 68

P

Paddler's Pub, 61
Partnership Shelter, 81
PATH, 207
Peaks of Otter, 97
Peck's Corner Shelter, 58
Pennsylvania, 13, 20, 23, 25, 31, 32, 33, 103, 123, 125, 128, 129, 133, 134, 135, 136, 138, 139, 140, 144, 179, 183, 188, 208, 209, 210
Petites Gap, 98
Philadelphia Trail Club, 209
Pilot Range, 155
Pine Grove Furnace State Park, 31, 131, 180, 208
Pine Knob Shelter, 127
Pine Swamp Branch Shelter, 89, 207
Pinnacles, 114
Pinwheel Vista, 164
Pisgah National Forest, 22
Plumorchard Gap Shelter, 42
Pochuck Mountain Shelter, 163
Potomac River, 125
Presidential Range, 155
Priest Shelter, 102
Priest Wilderness, 102
Pulpit Rock, 120, 139
Punch Bowl Shelter, 100

Q

Queen Anne's lace, 96

R

RAT, 207
Rice Field Shelter, 88
Roan Mountain, 63, 66, 67, 68, 69
Roaring Fork Shelter, 61
Rockfish Gap, 105, 106, 208
Rocky Gap, 90
Rocky Mountain, 40, 130, 177
Rod Hollow Shelter, 120
Round Mountain, 150

S

Saddle Trail, 173, 212
Sandwich Range, 155
Sandy Pond Trail, 173
Sarver Hollow Shelter, 90
Sassafras Gap Shelter, 49
SATC, 209
Schawangunk Mountains, 169
Schawangunk Ridge, 170
Seeley Woodworth Shelter, 102
Settlers Museum, 81, 82
Sharp Top Mountain, 94
Shenandoah Mountains, 113
Shenandoah National Park, 20, 109, 110, 114, 117, 133, 208
Shenandoah River, 122
Shook Branch Recreation Area, 72
Sierra Club, 193
Siler Bald Shelter, 47
Sinking Creek Mountain, 91
Sky Meadows State Park, 119
Skyland Lodge, 113
Skyline Drive, 95, 109
Sleeping Bag, 199
SMHC, 53, 206
Smoky Mountains, 20, 49, 51, 52, 54, 59, 61, 206
Snakes, 191
South Mountain, 34, 125, 126, 127, 140
South River Picnic Grounds, 111
Spivey Gap, 64, 206
Springer Mountain, 6, 15, 19, 20, 36, 206
Spy Rock, 102
Standing Indian Mountain, 45
Stone Man Mountain, 150
Stony Man Mountain, 113
Stratton mountains, 152
Susquehanna River, 129, 133, 134, 208
Symms Gap Meadow, 88

T

Tableland, 181
Taconic Range, 150
Tagg Run shelter, 32

TATC, 207
TEHCC, 206
Tennessee, 20, 22, 43, 51, 52, 54, 59, 63, 64, 66, 69, 70, 71, 73, 126, 206
Testnatee Gap, 176
The Ironmaster's Hostel, 31
The Place Hostel, 74
Thomas Knob, 78
Thoreau Spring, 181
Thru-Hikers' Companion, 27, 140, 141, 194
Tiorati Beach, 167
Tom Floyd Wayside Shelter, 116
Toms Run Shelters, 131
Torrington, 187
Trail Days, 74, 75, 78
Trail Names, 23
Tray Mountain, 40, 41, 177, 178
Trimpi Shelter, 80
Tumbling Run Shelter, 33, 179
Twinpeaks, 150

U

Unaba Mountain, 66
Uncle Johnny's Nolichucky Hostel, 64, 196
Upper Lake Cohasset, 168
US National Park Service, 109

V

Vandeventer Shelter, 72
Vermont, 13, 20, 22, 152, 153, 155, 210, 211

Virginia, 20, 22, 24, 29, 30, 74, 75, 76, 80, 82, 83, 85, 86, 88, 91, 92, 96, 97, 99, 105, 116, 117, 119, 120, 122, 123, 125, 126, 133, 183, 194, 206, 207, 208

W

Walker Mountain, 85, 86
Walker's Gap, 84
Washington Monument, 127
Watauga Dam, 72
Watauga Lake, 72
Watauga River, 72
Wawayanda Mountain, 164
Wayah Bald, 47
Wayah Gap, 47
West Virginia, 20, 88, 117, 126
White Mountain, 22, 76, 155
White Mountain National Forest, 22, 155
White Mountains, 21, 112, 155
White Rock, 90
White Rocks Mountain, 70
Wilburn Ridge, 79, 80
Wildcat Shelter, 164, 165
William Brien Memorial Shelter, 167
Wilmington Trail Club, 210
Wilson Creek Shelter, 94
Winding Stair Gap, 46
Wise Shelter, 79
Woods Hole Shelter, 38

Y

yellow loosestrife, 115
York Hiking Club, 208

Printed in the USA
CPSIA information can be obtained
at www.ICGtesting.com
LVHW050808021224
798088LV00001B/43